9/12

JUST AN OLD NAVY CUSTOM

JUST AN OLD NAVY CUSTOM

A. CECIL HAMPSHIRE

WILLIAM KIMBER · LONDON

First published in 1979 by
WILLIAM KIMBER & CO. LIMITED
Godolphin House, 22a Queen Anne's Gate,
London, SW1H 9AE

© A. Cecil Hampshire, 1979

ISBN 0 7183 0486 1

Photoset by
Specialised Offset Services Limited, Liverpool
and printed in Great Britain by
Redwood Burn, Trowbridge and Esher

Contents

List of Illustrations

Foreword

Thomas Ullock served in the Royal Navy as Purser and Paymaster from 1804 to 1860.

Throughout the early years of our naval history Pursers were perhaps the most abused of the officers, but not altogether with justice, since their supposed malpractices were frequently a consequence of the regulations of the time. The Purser was in fact made the scapegoat of other harpies who battened on the seamen.

Pursers were also maligned in other ways, not least that they were no great shakes as combatants. According to one distinguished historian: 'In action the Purser either retired to his berth below the waterline out of danger, or went to the cockpit to moisten the lips of the wounded with weak rum and water or lime juice.'

If this were true, then Thomas Ullock was a notable exception; and according to the history books he was very much a fighting man.

His first ship, which he joined as an unfledged clerk, was wrecked with considerable loss of life; he was promoted to Purser after only twelve months' service in the Navy; he served in China, the West Indies, and on the Lisbon and Mediterranean stations. In the Adriatic after the Battle of Trafalgar, where a British naval squadron was fully employed in thwarting Napoleon's attempts to enforce his 'Continental System', Ullock took part in numerous boat actions against the enemy, and was eventually severely wounded. Medical treatment was poor, but he continued to serve bravely and uncomplainingly. His only son was killed in Mexican waters while still a young midshipman.

Ullock served in war and peace, and from the days of sail to the coming of steam and ironclads. At the age of sixty-eight, although officially considered 'unfit for active service at sea', he still sought to continue in the Service he loved, and was in fact promised a post by the 'Sailor King', William IV. When he died at the age of seventy-six, the French musket ball which had cut him down in the Adriatic was still embedded in his thigh, never having been extracted.

Thomas Ullock was my maternal great-great-grandfather, and it is to him and all the sailors of past centuries from whom the British Navy's customs and traditions have been inherited, that this book is inscribed.

A.C.H.

CHAPTER I

Joining the 'Andrew'

If he could return to earth today, the old-time British sailor would be astounded by the changes which have been wrought in the Navy he knew, and baffled by the nuclear-powered and gas turbine-driven steel hulls packed with complex electronic gadgetry and weaponry which have replaced his oak-timbered, sail-propelled, muzzle loader-armed ship of the line. But 'the mainsheet, though in a different form, still drives the Queen's ships to windward',* and on board the modern counterparts of those 'wooden walls' of bygone years our old Tarpaulin can still hear much of the same familiar jargon he used, and note the continuance of customs, traditions and superstitions which have not changed in essence throughout the centuries.

He would discover that at least one verbal link with the hated recruiting methods of his day still remains. Perpetuating the memory of a legendary member of the press-gang who was said to have claimed ownership of the Navy because of the hundreds of

A modern guided missile destroyer.

* Admiral Sir Christopher Cradock, *Whispers from the Fleet.*

men he had pressed, since his christian name lives on in the Service his activities did not adorn, the Royal Navy is still known to the men of the lower deck as *the Andrew*.

Yet relevant records and old Navy Lists may be searched in vain for Andrew Miller, which is reputed to have been the man's full name, or 'tally'. In their heyday the press-gangs, whose head office once stood on Tower Hill, in London, numbered a good many naval officers seconded for this unpleasant duty, including for a spell even Nelson himself, although he thoroughly disapproved of the whole system. But the absence of the name of Andrew Miller from any surviving official record does not mean that there was no such zealous press-gangsman. HM Impress Service, the official title of what might be termed the old-time naval recruiting department, included in addition to real sailors, large numbers of civilians, who ranged from common labourer to street thug. One notorious press-gang, for example, included three farmers, a weaver and a bricklayer.

This method of providing a supply of manpower for Britain's sea service has a long and unsavoury history stretching back to Saxon times when it became a prerogative of the Crown. King John brought it into prominence when, soon after he had signed Magna Carta, he threatened to hang a number of Welsh merchants who failed to furnish men for his ships. In those days, and for some four hundred years to come, men were enlisted into the Navy by means of 'prest' money, or the King's shilling. Once the shilling had been accepted, however unwillingly, the recipient was considered to have entered into a contract to serve. The word *prest* comes from the French to loan or advance.

There were always of course some who volunteered to serve afloat. Boys joined the Navy to become man-of-war's-men, and remained so as long as they were fit for service, chiefly because they were never allowed to escape, and also because after a time there was no other calling open to them. Unaware of the hardships which had to be endured afloat, even by subordinate officers, many youths, excited by the stories of stirring sea fights, were keen to join. In a letter to Admiral Sir Edward Hawke after the Battle of Quiberon Bay in 1759, young Charles Manners wrote:

I hear you have beat the French fleet when they wer coming to kill us, and that one of your captains twisted a French ship round till it sunk. I wish you was coming home for I intend to go to sea if you will take me with you. I am Lord Granby's second son.

A good many men joined the Service from patriotic motives; speciously worded posters and glib recruiting agents promising plenty of prize money and unlimited grog drew a certain proportion into the Navy's net, as did the premiums and bounties which were constantly being offered as inducements. This recruiting poster, produced in the year 1770 when Britain was trying to raise a fleet to avenge the bombardment of the Falkland Islands by a Spanish squadron, is a typical example of these lures:

> All True Blue BRITISH HEARTS OF OAK who are able and no doubt willing to serve their God KING AND COUNTRY on board of His MAJESTY'S SHIPS are hereby invited to repair to the Roundabout Tavern, near New Crane, Wapping, where they will find Lieutenant JAMES AYSCOUGH of the *Bellona*, who still keeps his right real Senior, General and Royal Portsmouth Rendezvous for the Entertainment and Reception of such GALLANT SEAMEN who are proud to serve on board of the ships now lying at Portsmouth, Plymouth, Chatham and Sheerness.

Not only did Lieutenant Ayscough declare that he would be 'Damn'd happy to shake hands with any of his old shipmates in particular and their jolly friends in general', he offered a bounty of three pounds to volunteers, and conduct money and free transport for their chests, bedding, etc. A sinister footnote in small print at the bottom of the poster, however, added that 'for the encouragement of discovering seamen that may be impressed, a reward of Two Pounds will be given for Able, and Thirty Shillings for Ordinary Seamen'.

The Army, which had its own press-gangs, was also competing in the market for manpower, *vide* this poster seeking recruits for the Queen's Own Regiment of Light Dragoons:

> Young fellows whose hearts beat high to tread to Paths of Glory would not have better opportunity than now offers. Come forward then and enrole yourselves in a Regiment that stands

unrivalled, and where the kind of treatment the men ever experience is well known throughout the whole Kingdom. Each young hero, on being approved, will be allowed the largest bounty of Government.

A few smart lads will be taken at sixteen years of age, 5 feet 2 inches, but they must be active and well limbed.

Apply to Sergeant Hooker, Nag's Head, Norwich.

As an extra inducement the poster added: 'N.B. This Regiment is mounted on blood horses, and being lately returned from Spain and the horses young, the men will not be allowed to hunt during the next season *more than once a week*'.

One result of the Navy's preparations for hostilities in 1770, which did not in the event come to anything, the Spaniards having climbed down, was that young Horatio Nelson joined the ship commanded by his uncle, Captain Maurice Suckling, at Chatham.

But the vast majority of seamen were dragged neck and crop into the Service by the press-gangs, who knew a likely man the moment they set eyes on him. The best, of course, were taken out of merchant ships, usually those inward bound in the Channel and home waters, by sea gangs who formed, as it were, the outer ring of the net. Frequently they would practically denude a ship of her crew, so that it was almost impossible for the infuriated master to make his home port. When a warship had obtained a good nucleus of prime seamen, the vacancies remaining in complement were filled up with men who could be seized anyhow and anywhere. It was usually left to individual captains to obtain crews and get their ships to sea or forfeit their appointment.

No matter what the landsman's occupation, business or professional man, married or single, he was knocked on the head if he showed fight, and was carried aboard and remained there until the ship was paid off or a war was at an end.*

Local press-gangs usually set up their headquarters, called the 'Rendezvous' or 'Rondy', in any public house whose landlord was not averse to their presence, and hung a Union Jack from an upstairs window. Armed with cutlasses, or 'hangers', and oaken

* *The British Navy*, Protheroe.

clubs, the gangs roamed the streets of most seaport towns. 'Landsmen' were officially exempted from pressing, but such exemptions were frequently ignored. Males under the age of eighteen and over fifty-five were also exempt; but since they were required to prove their age, it was often too late by the time this could be done.

Any irregularity in the description of the holder of a protection certificate was sufficient to warrant seizure during a 'hot press'. One apprentice – another exempted class of citizen – was described on his certificate as 'smooth-faced', meaning beardless. Nevertheless he was swept into the net because he was pock-marked and thus according to the heartless impress officer could not be smooth-faced!

> Likely victims were even seized at the church door whence bridegroom and congregation were carried off. As it was such a common spectacle of the times, eighteenth-century children often amused themselves by playing at 'press-gangs'.†

In the early eighteenth century Navy men could press the crews of merchantmen for 'impudence', which involved such lubberly behaviour as not dousing the topsail, or dipping colours – considered a gross contempt of the King's Service' – flying his Majesty's Jack, or hoisting colours the wrong way up. Collisions were similarly punished. When Queen Anne authorised the impressment of musicians, since there had to be some fun on shipboard, one naval captain pressed a blind man because he could play the Irish bagpipes. But this was too much for the authorities. The man was ordered to be discharged and the captain charged up with the cost of his pay and victuals! Being tattoed brought one within the scope of the press-gangs since this method of adornment was especially popular with seafaring men; as also did the physical peculiarity of bow-legs – thus many tailors were pressed. Even women were sometimes pressed, and in 1806 a Lieutenant McKee, who commanded the local Sea Fencibles at Portland, rated his daughter midshipman.

John Scott, a farm labourer of Mistley, in Suffolk, was working in

† *English Social History*, Trevelyan.

The press-gang at work.
Eighteenth-century children playing at 'Press-gangs'.

the fields in his shirtsleeves when he was seized, although his protection certificate was in his coat pocket a few yards away. Three inebriated Falmouth men who tossed bottles and other objects on to the stage of a theatre to mark their appreciation of the performance were promptly pressed. As late as 1804 a gang, headed by a naval captain, broke into the house of William Trim, a seafaring man of Poole. Trim seized a red hot poker to defend himself, but he was overpowered. His sister was assaulted, and his 70-year-old father who rushed to his help was stabbed and beaten.

Press-gangs were not infrequently used by the unscrupulous for their own ends. John Stilwell of Clerkenwell was legatee to a small fortune held in trust by his stepmother and uncle. To remove this unwelcome obstacle to their financial expectations they had him pressed as an 'incorrigible son'. The harbourmaster of Ramsgate wanted to get rid of William Taylor, a local fisherman who was courting his daughter. He had him pressed.

But the gangs did not always have things their own way, for by and large the populace detested them. At Leith a small group of townspeople, encouraged by their baillie, called at the local 'Rondy' one night and asked to have a last drink with some friends who had been pressed. After being incautiously admitted, they threw spirits on to the fire which caused a blaze, and in the subsequent confusion released the victims. There were even sham press-gangs, but occasionally Nemesis would catch up with these, and they would find themselves pressed in their turn by a real gang!

Unhappily everyone was after the seafaring man. Police and road users reported him, and mistresses betrayed him, for he was always worth twenty shillings, the official price as a 'straggler', and conduct money to get him to the ship. Until the abolition of pay ledgers in the Royal Navy and their replacement by a computerised pay system in the 1970s, charges for 'straggling' – the old-time expenses for the recovery of deserters – were still allowed for against a sailor's account.

Towards the end of the eighteenth century, as the wars in which Britain was involved grew wider in extent and the demand for ships and crews more imperative, neither bounties nor the utmost efforts of the press-gangs could provide sufficient men for the Royal Navy. Quota Acts were passed, compelling each county and seaport to furnish a specified number of men according to size and population. But local authorities took advantage of the Acts to rid their districts of gipsies, poachers and other undesirables of every description, who were useless at sea. Such men were known as 'King's Hard Bargains', or, in the case of offenders from London who had been given the option by the City's magistrates of going to prison or joining the Navy, 'My Lord Mayor's Men'. Thus the quota schemes proved a failure.

By then an official Impress Service had come into being, commanded by regular naval officers appointed for specific periods with the title of 'Regulating Captain', and depots set up all over Britain where seafarers congregated. Edinburgh and Leith, for example, had a gang twenty-one strong, which included two lieutenants and four midshipmen. Other depots were set up at Greenock, Liverpool, Newcastle, Great Yarmouth, Milford Haven, Cowes, Deal, Dover and Folkestone. Their 'catches' were despatched to special receiving ships at the home ports, from whence the men were packed off to seagoing vessels of the Fleet. So important was this work that at one time no less than twenty-four captains and fifty-six lieutenants were fully employed. The legendary Andrew Miller may well have been one of these.

Between the Peace of Amiens in 1802 and the resumption of war with Napoleon in the following year, thousands of men deserted from the Royal Navy, and it was not easy to make good these numbers. Ordered to conduct a 'hot press' in the West Country, the captain of HMS *Venerable* reported gloomily to the Admiralty:

> In pursuance of your order, I went last night to Dartmouth with the officers and men previously directed, and made a strict search in all the Public Houses, and in every other place where the Lieutenant of the Rendezvous thought there might be a probability of success; I despatched at the same time a party to examine all the vessels afloat. I am sorry to say the result of these endeavours only produced two men; this is, I imagine, to be accounted for by the same duty having been several times performed at Dartmouth since the first breaking out of the Impress, which has made the seamen too wary to be suddenly caught; indeed, I am informed that the greater part of them are retired some miles into the country, particularly at the back of

Teignmouth, where nothing but an adequate Military force can insure their being secured for his Majesty's Service.

Perhaps this handbill proved a more effective draw in London and the Home Counties:

Who would enter for small craft, when the *Leander*, the finest frigate in the world, with a good spar deck overhead to keep you dry, warm and comfortable, and a lower deck like a barn, where you may play at leap-frog when the hammocks are hung up, has still room for a hundred active seamen, and a dozen stout lads for yardsmen. This whacking double-banked frigate is fitting at Woolwich, to be flag-ship on the fine, healthy, full-bellied Halifax station, where you may get a bushel of potatoes for a shilling, a cod fish for a biscuit, and a glass of boatswain's grog for twopence. Lots of leave on shore; dancing and fiddling on board, and four pounds of tobacco served out every month. A few strapping fellows who would eat an enemy alive are wanted for Admiral's bargemen.

It was not that British seamen lacked patriotism: their reluctance was chiefly due to the conditions of service in the Navy, even with the reforms introduced after the mutinies of 1797. 'Life on board by modern standards was execrable. Ill-fed, ill-housed, ill-clothed and ill-paid, he (the sailor) was a victim of the age he lived in'.*

Although its activities ceased after the end of the Napoleonic wars, HM Impress Service finally died quietly and unmourned in 1833. The reasons for its demise were the demoralising effect it had upon the nation as a whole, discontent in the Navy, exasperation among the leaders of trade and industry, and public outcry generally. Also, with the end of the Napoleonic wars the nation entered upon an era of peace and prosperity. Impressment had proved expensive, for the cost of a volunteer was a mere thirty shillings; that of a pressed man anything up to £100 or more.

In 1835, with the 'Sailor King' William IV on the throne, an effort was made to man the Navy entirely by voluntary recruitment. In August of that year an act was passed 'for the encouragement of

* *The British Sailor – A Social History*, Kemp, (Dent 1970).

voluntary enlistment of seamen and to make regulations for more effectually manning his Majesty's Navy'. Thus men would be entered for five years, but they could be retained for an additional six months or until the end of a period of emergency. They were to be given certificates of service, and at the end of the five years, protection from impressment for a period of two years. But if they were discharged before the expiration of five years, they would be given protection for one year only. If a man was discharged before the end of five years, he was to provide two landsmen or one able seaman to serve in his stead. Men were entered for a particular ship of their own choice, served for one commission only and were then discharged. The act applied equally to 'colonials'.

Unfortunately even these inducements failed of their purpose. When a sudden crisis blew up with France over Syria in 1840, it took four months to raise the crews required to man a number of reinforcements for the Mediterranean Fleet. In 1852, therefore, an Admiralty Committee was set up to examine the whole question of manning the Navy.

The committee produced its report in the following February, and an Order-in-Council was issued on 1st April instituting continuous service for the lower deck. The scheme now produced – its author one Charles Pennell, a senior clerk of the Admiralty who was later knighted – was for boys to be entered for ten years' continuous service and general service from the age of eighteen, and men who thereafter entered the Navy for the first time. All were to serve for ten years, with increased rates of pay. Seamen who had served, or were at present serving, and who volunteered to re-enter, or continue to serve under the new conditions, would receive the new pay rates, and certain portions of their previous service would be allowed to count towards the ten years. After ten years they would receive a pension of sixpence a day, or more if they joined the body of experienced seamen held available to train raw ships' companies.

The rating of leading seaman was introduced, and that of landsman abolished and replaced by that of ordinary seaman second class. A new rating of chief petty officer was established for the Master-at-Arms, Chief Boatswain's Mate, Chief Captain of the Forecastle, Admiral's Coxswain, Chief Quartermaster, Chief Carpenter's Mate, Seamen's Schoolmaster, Ship's Steward and

Ship's Cook. There were other improvements in pay and conditions of service, and it was recommended that barracks should be built on shore to replace the old receiving ships.

The Times commented approvingly:

> No one will grudge the small expense (£55,000 annually in pay alone) required to support our maritime establishment on a proper footing and put an end to the absurd practice of dispersing a body of seamen just at the moment they attain the highest degree of efficiency.

But at first seamen were still hard to get. When the Fleet was being prepared for war with Russia in 1853, Lord Clarence Paget writing of his appointment to the 91-gun *Princess Royal*, recorded that:

> There was a scarcity, indeed almost an absence, of seamen. However, with the assistance of several valuable officers who were appointed to the ship, and by dint of handbills and touting of all sorts, we managed to enter at the average of 20 to 30 a week, such as they were. Scarcely any of them had been in a man-of-war and consequently they were entirely ignorant of the management of great guns and muskets. I had named 1st March (1854) as the earliest period I could get the ship to Spithead, but the Admiralty were so anxious to make a show that we were forced out on 15th February, and a very pretty mess we made of it. But we still could not get men, men, men! I wrote and wrote to the Admiralty stating that if they did not assist me by placing 200 coastguards on board I should be taken by the first Russian frigate we fell in with.

Yet in 1857, after the end of the Crimean War, no fewer than 3,000 seamen were allowed to cancel their engagements. Later the Admiralty had to offer bounties to make up deficiencies.

Thus, although impressment was discontinued more than a century ago – yet never actually abolished – having long been replaced by the voluntary system, higher pay and greatly improved conditions of service, the bad old times are still unwittingly recalled by the sailor of today when he refers to his Service by the christian name of a long-forgotten press-gangsman.

CHAPTER II

All 'Harry Tate's' and 'Ticklers'

Ask an old naval man for his opinion of the Service today and the odds are that he will mutter darkly – and perhaps with a touch of envy – that 'it doesn't blow like it used to'. By this he means that conditions of life afloat since his days have changed out of all recognition. The remark also has a more truly nautical connotation.

High winds whip up rough seas, and these in their turn bring considerable discomfort afloat, and not infrequently in the past, actual hazards for sailors – even in twentieth-century warships, particularly those that were coal-burning. In fact, life was so uncomfortable in the Navy's early destroyers, submarines and other small warships wherein living quarters were cramped, that Winston Churchill, who once went to sea in a destroyer for the experience soon after his appointment as First Lord of the Admiralty prior to the outbreak of the First World War, prised from a reluctant Treasury the payment of a special allowance, known as 'Hard Lying Money', to compensate small-ship sailors for the discomforts they were called upon to endure at sea. Hard Lying Money, or 'Hard Lyers', continues to be paid right up to the present day 'to personnel in those ships employed mainly in open waters where living conditions are markedly below those which can be expected in a modern frigate'.

Pressed to expatiate further on the theme of change, our old sailor might well go on to lament that the Navy he loved despite its faults seems to be 'all Harry Tate's', and that life for the present-day 'matlow' (his pronunciation of the French *matelot*) is one long 'banyan'.

The first reference is almost too recent to require explanation. Harry Tate was a music-hall comedian, well known in the days when motor-cars were still something of a novelty, the highlight of whose stage performances was a riotous motoring sketch. With

Harry Tate's stage car nothing worked properly, and his antics in trying to get the thing to function had his audiences rolling in the aisles. In 1912, along with a host of other theatrical stars, he appeared at the Palace Theatre, Shaftesbury Avenue, in the first Royal Variety Command Performance ever held. Before an appreciative audience, which included King George V and Queen Mary, he performed his *tour de force* which was, of course, the famous motoring sketch. This nautical expression, therefore, dates back only a comparatively few years, and to sailors it means that discipline is slack, a ship is slovenly, and nothing works properly.

It has in fact become traditional for the term 'Harry Tate's' to be applied to any 'irregular' naval formation, such as, for example, the wartime Royal Naval Patrol Service. This 'navy within the Navy', formed in 1939 to perform minesweeping and anti-submarine duties, was composed chiefly of trawlers requisitioned from the fishing industry and hastily converted into minor warships. Manned by ex-fishermen, volunteer reservists and 'Hostilities Only' officers and men who came from all walks of life, the cheerful disregard by the crews of this 'Lilliput Fleet' of the niceties of naval procedure and discipline was apt at times to drive senior officers of the regular Navy to the brink of apoplexy. It did not, however, detract in any way from their courage and efficiency. Other 'Harry Tate' organisations of the Second World War included Combined Operations, the Levant Schooner Flotilla – a polyglot force which included members of all three services and distinguished itself against the enemy in the Aegean – and the Special Boat Squadron: in fact, any sort of 'private navy'.

But our old Tar's reference to life in the modern Royal Navy being 'one long banyan' is very early navalese indeed, for the term recalls a much hated practice concerned with victualling afloat, although by a typical nautical inversion of meaning, it has today come to signify exactly the opposite. To discover its origin, therefore, we must go back in time at least to the Tudor Navy.

In the reign of Henry VIII, who, aside from his propensity for acquiring wives in his quest for a son to succeed him, has a valid claim to be regarded as the 'Father' of Britain's sea service along with King Alfred, the sailor's basic ration scale as officially laid down consisted of one pound of biscuit and one gallon of beer every day, and '200 pieces of flesh to every 100 men' on four days a week.

Beer had for long been a recognised right, and despite the fact that it was often vile stuff because of poor quality in the first place and the difficulty of keeping it on shipboard, the seaman insisted on his daily potion of 'Poor John'. In this respect, however, the British sailor was no different from his fellow-man ashore. Before the advent of tea and coffee in England, ale was drunk at every meal, even by children, since the drinking water was often impure. On board ship fresh water quickly went bad. Vice-Admiral Lovell, writing about conditions in his own flagship as late as the year 1800, noted that 'the water was so putrid, thick and stinking, that I often held my nose with one hand while I drank it strained through my pocket handkerchief'. A gallon of beer a day was not therefore an excessive amount, and, from a medical standpoint, good sound beer was an excellent anti-scorbutic.

Henry's daughter, the first Queen Elizabeth, made few changes in these rations. But the meat allowance, either fresh or salt, was now fixed at two pounds per man, while half a pound of butter six times in a month of twenty-eight days and the same amount of cheese were added. It will be seen that already the Crown was guilty of sharp practice, since the lunar month only was used for both the sailor's pay and victuals. On the days when meat was not issued, known officially as 'fast days', the sailor was entitled to one and a half pounds of salt fish. He was thus brought into line with civilians ashore, for Queen Elizabeth caused a number of 'fish laws' to be passed, ordering the observance by the populace of 'Fish Days'. Thus none of her subjects were allowed to eat meat during Lent or on Fridays – sometimes Wednesdays were added. The purpose of these decrees was 'to maintain Britain's seafaring population, to revive decayed coast towns, and to prevent the too great consumption of beef and mutton which resulted in the conversion of arable land into pasture'.*

As time went on victualling for the Fleet continued to remain almost unaltered, except that the salt beef issue could now be varied by bacon or pork. Pickled in brine and packed in harness casks, the meat was often merely bone and gristle; the sailors contemptuously termed it 'junk' since that is what it resembled in appearance and texture. Junk was old and decaying rope. By the time the cheese was issued it was frequently so hard that the sailors

* *English Social History*, Trevelyan.

carved it into buttons for their jackets and trousers, snuff boxes and other fancy articles in their spare time.

Not only was meat not issued on three days a week: during the Continental wars which spanned the greater part of the eighteenth century, the British Fleet was almost continuously at sea fighting our enemies in various parts of the world. Due to lack of adequate storage facilities, the sailor's rations were then frequently subject to further reduction 'according to the exigence of the Service'. This generally took the form of making the rations for four men suffice for six, which gave rise to the contemporary expression, 'living six upon four'. To compensate the men 'Short Allowance Money' was ordered to be paid to them, but this edict was more often honoured in the breach rather than the observance by the ship's purser, known to all for reasons touched on later, as 'Mister Nipcheese'.

This particular aspect of a seaman's life was happily expressed in rhyme in 1671 by John Baltharpe, a former sailor turned poet:

> *What meat before the King for four*
> *Allow'd, now six men it devour;*
> *A dollar to each man is due,*
> *Each twenty and eight days 'tis true;*
> *When we can get it, we drink wine,*
> *Healths to their friends then we combine.*
> *A seaman when he gets ashoar,*
> *In one day's time he spendeth more*
> *Than three months' short allowance money.*

Officers, too, were similarly compelled to go short of victuals, or exist on 'bare Navy' when ships were on active service and there was insufficient food to go round. On such days their traditional grace before meals was changed to: 'Messing three among four of us, thank God there aren't more of us'. When reduced still further and they were forced to subsist on half rations, the grace ran: 'Messing four among two of us, thank God there are but few of us'.

Sailors were denied meat on Mondays, Wednesdays and Fridays, and accordingly they dubbed these 'Banyan days'. This term was derived from an East Indian sect who would not kill any animal or eat flesh. The usual dress worn by these people was a loose flowing garment known as a *banian*. So widespread did this nautical expression become that it soon found its way on shore.

> The sailor was always an object of attraction and interest to his fellows when he returned from his voyages and told them his wondrous tales. Thus it was that the language of the sea descended into the speech of the people, being employed to describe nearly every vicissitude and condition to which human nature is heir.*

The term even turned up in the eighteenth-century theatre. A popular farce of the time in two acts by a playwright named George Brewer was actually called *Bannian Day*. With songs and appropriate nautical colour, the scene was laid in Plymouth. In the plot a gentleman's son, a lieutenant in the Navy, marries a lady without fortune and is disowned by his father. The young officer eventually finds himself in low water due to lack of funds, his condition being described as suffering from *bannian day*. But the hero, appropriately named Jack Hawser, brings about a reconciliation between the lieutenant's wife and her father-in-law, whose prejudices are overcome and he makes atonement. In the finale Jack Hawser declaims in song that: 'All I hope is that the *Bannian Day* of every messmate in distress may end as happily as ours.'

The earliest reference in official documents in the Navy to *banyan*, or *banian* day, appeared in 1669 in the narrative of an officer of HMS *St David*, flagship of Admiral Sir John Harman, Commander-in-Chief of the Mediterranean Fleet. The expression, which also appeared in Nelson's despatches, was frequently used to denote a famishing time.

Today, however, as has been remarked, the term has come to mean a feast, a party, or any kind of a good time, preferably with everything provided free, or 'all Harry Freeman's'. This inversion of meaning came about when sailors began to save up odds and ends from their daily rations in order to make delicacies to be enjoyed on fast days.

And who, it might be asked, is or was Harry Freeman? This naval expression dates back to the London of long ago, and is said to have been derived from an old-time Cockney remark about

---

* *The British Tar in Fact and Fiction*, Robinson.

'drinking at Freeman's quay'. Henry Freeman was in fact an eighteenth-century warehouse owner of Tooley Street, near Tower Bridge, who provided free beer to the porters who worked for him. Possibly some press-ganged Londoner in the days of Andrew Miller brought the expression into the Navy with him, and it has remained current to this day to denote something obtained for nothing.

Meatless days in the Navy were officially ended in 1824. In June of that year an Order-in-Council established a new and improved scale of victualling for the Fleet. The order stated that:

> There shall be allowed to every Person serving in his Majesty's ships the following daily quantities of provisions, viz – Bread, one pound; Beer, one gallon; Cocoa, one ounce; Sugar, one and a half ounces; Fresh meat, one pound; Vegetables, half a pound; Tea, quarter of an ounce; and Weekly, Oatmeal, half a pint; Vinegar, half a pint. Flag Officers, Captains and other Commanding Officers will observe the above scale and will fully explain to the Ships' Companies under their orders the advantages of the new system, viz, that what were called *banyan days* are abolished; that Meat with vegetables, Flour or Pease, is to be issued every day; that Flour instead of being exchanged for a portion of Beef, will now become an article of the Men's regular allowance, and that a quantity of Tea or Coffee, sufficient to make a pint of liquid, will be issued every evening.

Food has always been important to the sailor, being after pay the second of his basic wants, as Samuel Pepys knew well when he held the post of Surveyor-General of the Victualling.

> Englishmen, and more especially seamen, [he remarked] love their bellies above anything else, and therefore it must always be remembered in the management of the victualling of the Navy, that to make any abatement from them in the quantity or agreeableness of the Victuals is to discourage and provoke them in the tenderest point, and will sooner render them disgusted with the King's service than any other one hardship that can be put upon them.

And Pepys should have known! He it was who first regularised Navy victualling and worked out the first comprehensive table of rations, which were varied and nutritious for the time.

Even so, they still left much to be desired, judging from a heartcry written by the captain of HMS *Ann and Christopher* at Sheerness to the Navy Board in January 1675, soon after the end of the Third Dutch War:

> Vitules sent us heer on board is not fit for his Mates Servies porke very small nothing but Raine and bones when it is boyled ... beare worse then water, they doe but spoill good water in breuing such, my men doth grumble verey much att the vitules.
>
> Signed John Votear. Commander

In those early days, and in fact right up to the end of the nineteenth century, the sailor's rations had been made more unappetising because of the poor quality of the cooking. Naval cooks were then recruited from Greenwich pensioners or men unfit for other ratings. The ship's cook – incidentally, he did not cook for the captain, who brought his own cook along with the rest of his private retinue – had little more to do than steep the daily issue of salt junk in a tub until it became softer and more pliable. It was then boiled for several hours until the men were piped to dinner, when it was served out to the different messes. Half the slush skimmed from the coppers became the cook's perquisite, and half went to the boatswain for grease. In return for tobacco or other favours the cook's half was often traded to the sailors for use in making duffs, or puddings. Small wonder that scurvy was prevalent afloat, until eventually in 1826 the Admiralty ordered the practice to be discontinued, 'as scarcely anything is more unwholesome or more likely to produce scurvy'. Small wonder, too, that the expression 'Sea Cook' became an epithet of contempt. The latter's assistant was usually known as 'Jack Nastyface'.

Breakfast in the days of Britain's 'wooden walls' consisted of 'burgoo', an unpopular mixture made of coarse oatmeal boiled in water and sweetened with molasses when available. Today this term is still applied in the Navy to any form of porridge, albeit that the latter is very far removed in every respect from the unsavoury mess which the Navy knew up to the end of last century. 'Scotch coffee' was often preferred to 'burgoo'; this was simply burnt bread boiled in water and sweetened with sugar.

Naval ship's cook of the seventeenth century. They were often crippled and maimed pensioners of the Chatham Chest.

Twenty years after Trafalgar cocoa was introduced for breakfast in lieu of 'burgoo', and in 1832 was replaced by soluble chocolate. Manufactured in the Royal Victoria Victualling Yard at Deptford – the Navy's main 'larder' for some two hundred years – the beverage was made with cocoa beans from Grenada, Trinidad and Guayaquil in fixed proportions. The beans were roasted, crushed, mixed with sugar and arrowroot, pressed and stamped out in large thick slabs. Known to generations of sailors as *kye*, Navy chocolate makes a splendid drink, and has fortified many night watchmen and others, both officers and men, at sea and in harbour, from those early days right up to the present time. Today Navy chocolate, the ingredients of which remain unchanged, is manufactured by commercial firms since Deptford's historic victualling yard no longer exists but forms part of a Thames-side housing estate.

A glance at the place during its heyday after being moved down from Tower Hill in 1750 reveals some of its ramifications. In addition to the cocoa bean roasters and chocolate grinding mills, the Yard boasted its own abattoir and brine sheds where fresh meat was killed, salted down and packed in casks for issue to the Fleet. During the salting season an average of 500 beasts were slaughtered. Most of this meat was American beef and Danish and Irish pork. Soap and candles were manufactured and stocked in huge quantities; there were oat and flour mills, and the rum stores. One of the great oaken blending vats held as much as 32,817 gallons of rum, but was practically destroyed during the London blitz. The Yard, which was named after herself by Queen Victoria when she visited Deptford in 1858, was finally closed in 1961 and its remaining functions transferred to other victualling yards at the home ports.

In 1903 the recommendations of a committee on naval rations, chaired by the aptly named Vice-Admiral Rice, came into effect. The hated oatmeal was finally abolished; lower deck meals were increased from three to five daily; and items such as jams, marmalade and condensed milk added to the official ration scale. It may surprise many to learn, however, that salt pork continued to be issued in the British Fleet as late as 1926.

Eating and drinking afloat have given rise over the years to a good many peculiar naval terms and expressions, being periodically added to with the passage of time and the introduction of fresh items of food. Thus 'dandy funk' was once a popular naval dish. This was a kind of pudding or cake made by crushing ship's biscuits into powder and mixing this with molasses, adding water and baking the result. Chopped meat could also be used instead of molasses. Dandy funk, which has no modern equivalent, was one of the more palatable ways to consume the old-time ship's biscuit.

As a substitute for bread, biscuits were issued in the Navy from the very earliest times. First purchased commercially, then manufactured in the Royal victualling yards, they were thick, well browned, and stamped with a perforator so that the centre was more compressed and therefore tougher than the remainder. Usually the last piece eaten, this was called a 'reefer's nut'. Known universally as 'hard tack' – even the road leading to the biscuit bakery in the Deptford victualling yard where most of them were manufactured was known as 'Hard Tack Lane' – most ships' biscuits were made of mixed wheat and pea flour, with sometimes a base addition of bone dust. The pea flour generally worked itself into yellow lumps and veins of incredible hardness which could not be bitten through until the biscuit had become soft through long keeping. When it did become soft it acquired an unpleasant musty, sourish taste, and had begun to attract or breed weevils. These had to be knocked out before the biscuit could be eaten. A contemporary nautical way of expressing comfort was 'as snug as a maggot in the bread room'.

When the Duke of Edinburgh, Queen Victoria's second son, who served in the Navy and eventually became an Admiral of the Fleet, was a midshipman in the steam screw frigate *Euryalus* in the 1860s, the 'young gentlemen', like the rest of the ship's company, had to live on 'hard tack'. After duly expelling the weevils from their biscuits, the irrepressible midshipmen kept these creatures in pill-boxes, to be specially fed and trained and raced along the mess table in the weekly 'Maggot Derby'.

As the Navy's victualling began to improve, new terms were coined for various dishes, the generic slang name for which became 'scran'. 'Lobscouse', familiar also to men of the Merchant Navy, and in particular those who served in ships manned from Liverpool (hence the term 'Scouse' for a Liverpudlian), was a dish consisting of minced salt beef stewed with vegetables, and biscuits added.

Another popular dish was 'Oosh' or 'Open Air Pie'. This consisted of diced meat together with onions and other vegetables, seasoned and baked in an oven. 'Oosh', or more properly 'Hoosh', is in fact an Eskimo word, and the dish was introduced into the Navy by sailors who had served in the ships which from time to time since the beginning of last century were despatched in search of the elusive North-West Passage. When the British Schools' Exploring Society was started in 1932 by Surgeon-Commander Murray Levick, a naval dietetics expert who had served as medical officer and zoologist with Captain Scott on his last Antarctic expedition, *hoosh* was always included as part of the young explorers' ration scale, since it could be prepared and cooked by the boys themselves while roughing it in the wilds. Another slang term for this naval all-purpose stew was 'Potmess'.

In the early 1900s a form of 'general messing' copied from that which had recently been adopted in the United States Navy was tried out in the Royal Navy. Under this system the planning and preparation of all meals became the responsibility of the ship's supply officer, who also drew up weekly menus and arranged for the purchase and provision of all food stocks. But it was not popular with British sailors, and because of the difficulty of operating the system in small ships such as destroyers with limited galley and storage facilities, the Navy's former 'standard messing' was continued except in boys' shore training establishments. Under the latter system, which remained in force in most seagoing British warships well into the 1930s, the staple items of fare in the sailor's daily ration, such as meat, potatoes, bread and flour, were issued in bulk direct to messes as in sailing warship days, together with such other official provisions as tea, sugar and condensed milk.

Supplied in carcass, the fresh meat was cut up into unscientific joints by a Royal Marine 'butcher', or a volunteer seaman in ships which did not carry a Marine detachment, before being served out to individual messes. The only vegetables available, more often than not, were merely potatoes and dried peas. The actual meals were then prepared by 'cooks of the mess' and taken to the coal-fired galley for cooking. Since ships' cook ratings were then still comparatively untrained, about all they had to do was keep an eye on the various offerings brought along by the different messes. Judging by the results, they worked to a simple formula, maintained the disgusted sailors, of 'when 'em brown 'em done, when 'em black 'em mucked up!' The ingredients for breakfast and supper meals had to be obtained on repayment from the ship's stores or bought from the canteen, and prepared and cooked by the men themselves.

Since few sailors possessed the culinary expertise to do more than boil an egg, their efforts at preparing the midday meal rarely progressed beyond 'Straight rush'. This meant that the meat – often more bone than flesh – was simply placed in a dish, sprinkled by way of seasoning with the contents of a dry-packeted commercial product known as 'Edwards Desiccated Soup', or 'EDS', obtained from the canteen but seldom actually made into soup, and 'rushed' straight to the galley. 'Straight rush' was sometimes known as 'schooner on the rocks' when the joint rested on peeled potatoes.

The cooked result, swimming in the natural fat from the meat, since no one knew how or was prepared to try, to make gravy can be imagined. Crudely hacked into individual portions, rather than carved since he only had a jack-knife for the purpose, and served, or 'whacked out', to individuals by the mess cook, or senior hand, it usually had to be helped down by the liberal application of a pungent sauce known as 'Ally Slopers' which was stocked in most naval canteens. The sole direction on the manufacturer's label for the use of this popular condiment read simply: 'Take plenty with everything'. The cynical and irreverent maintained that this all-purpose sauce could even be used for polishing brightwork!

Since knives and forks, or 'port and starboard oars', were usually in short supply in most seamen's messes, his working knife had to do duty as an eating implement. As mentioned in a later chapter, knives and forks for the men of the lower deck became an official issue in 1907. Prior to this date, only spoons had been supplied by the Admiralty, but some canteen contractors loaned eating utensils to individual messes.

When the allotted joint of meat lent itself to stewing, a more ambitious 'cook of the mess' might try his hand at preparing an 'oosh' or 'potmess'; while those individuals who prided themselves on their skill at making pastry, or 'clacker', covered the dish with a pie crust, the resultant creation then being known as 'oosh with an awning'. Except in the case of a 'straight rush' or 'schooner on the rocks', the potatoes and peas were separately steamed for each mess in crude string nets, the latter emerging bullet-hard and tasteless.

Breakfast and supper items of food attracted their own peculiar nicknames. Thus a kipper became a 'Spithead pheasant', a 'deep sea' or 'one-eyed steak'; tinned tomatoes, supplied and eaten as an accompaniment to bacon, were known as 'red lead'; tinned herrings in tomato sauce became simply 'herrings in'; sardines were dubbed 'whales'; and meat pasties known universally as 'tiddy-oggies'. Brawn rejoiced in the sombre nickname of 'railway smash'.

Any kind of tinned meat, or corned beef, was dubbed 'corned dog', 'Admiralty ham'; sometimes 'Seventeen west' or 'Dead west' to indicate that the meat probably came originally from across the Atlantic. At first the issue of preserved meat in the Navy was restricted to sick sailors serving on foreign stations as a special diet, or medical comfort. Tried out experimentally in ships employed on the East and West Indies stations in 1813, it was known officially as 'soup and bouilli', and was the first 'bully beef'. Eventually it became a standard item in the Navy's ration scale as a substitute for salt beef on one day of the week.

In 1867 the Royal Victoria Yard began to issue tinned mutton to warships at Portsmouth on a trial basis. Although an excellent product, it did not find favour with the sailors. In that year a particularly gruesome crime attracted considerable publicity in local newspapers in the Portsmouth area as well as the national press. A 29-year old solicitor's clerk named Frederick Baker of Alton, in Hampshire, had enticed a nine-year-old girl named Fanny Adams away from her playmates and murdered her. He then dismembered her body, even cutting out her eyes and heart, severing her arms and legs, and 'cleaning the bowels out of the body like a chicken'. The fragments were scattered about in a field and some found in a nearby stream. Baker kept a diary in which he actually recorded this appalling deed. He was duly arrested and brought to trial, found guilty and hanged at Winchester.

The sailors thereupon dubbed the new and unpopular issue of tinned mutton 'Fanny Adams', and a colloquialism was born. Oddly enough, once a handle had been wired to the top, the tin in which the meat was supplied lent itself to various domestic uses on shipboard, such as, for instance, a receptacle in which to draw the mess's daily rum ration. The Admiralty took the hint, the corned mutton was withdrawn, and in due course a new lower deck mess utensil made its appearance in the Fleet to replace the old and cumbersome wooden 'kit'. Not surprisingly, it was known as a 'fanny'.

When jam was first added to the Navy's official ration it was supplied by a firm called Tickler and Company of London. Around this time, when the Earl of Selborne was First Lord of the Admiralty, he and Admiral Fisher, then the First Sea Lord, introduced a new type of short service engagement for sailors in order to provide a Fleet Reserve. Entered for seven years' active service and five in the Reserve, the new recruits were called by regular Navy men 'Selborne's Light Horse'. Scornfully the older shellbacks suggested that the new issue of jam was obviously intended for the short service men who could not be expected to eat proper sailor's food. Both they as well as the jam now became known as 'Ticklers'.

This new issue was followed by the introduction of tinned tobacco for those who cared to take it up in lieu of the leaf tobacco which had been the only kind hitherto supplied. Once again the old-timers swore that this fancy tobacco was intended for the 'Ticklers' who would not serve long enough afloat to learn the art of chewing it, and dubbed it 'Ticklers' tobacco'. Subsequently both Navy tinned tobacco and the cigarettes rolled from it came to be called 'Ticklers'. Commercially manufactured cigarettes were termed 'tailor-mades'.

The old-time purser had been allowed to sell quantities of 'cut and dried, sweet-scented tobacco' to the men up to an individual amount of two pounds a month at a rate settled by the Navy Board. Brought over in casks from Virginia, and examined for quality at the Royal Victoria Yard, it was complete with leaf and stalk. When issued on board ship the men made it up into *periques*, which could be either smoked in a pipe or chewed. Since smoking was restricted to the galley space because of the danger of fire, chewing was more often preferred. This gave rise to the nautical expression 'making a dead man chew', and was yet another attack on the integrity of that much maligned individual, the purser. It meant that he was guilty of claiming repayment from the Admiralty for tobacco issued to a deceased or non-existent rating.

In fact, the purser could be said to have been encouraged in such a practice since he was entitled to bear on his muster book two fictitious seamen known as 'Widows' Men' to every hundred in the ship's company. This was in pursuance of Acts of Parliament passed in 1735 and 1751, their pay and allowances being paid into a fund for the relief of officers' widows. In order that a check might be kept on the purser in this respect, a special evolution was introduced into ships of the Fleet, to be carried out periodically. Known as 'mustering by the open list', this required every member of the ship's company to step forward in front of the captain at a special parade and state his name and rating, and, with the later introduction of pay ledgers afloat, the special qualifications for which he was entitled to receive extra pay. The captain thus satisfied himself that all was in order, and that more men were not borne than appeared in the Muster Book. Subsequently this evolution came to be used as a form of personal inspection by a flag officer.

Because smokers used to congregate companionably in the galley to smoke their pipes and yarn together, most rumours originated there and were known as 'galley packets'. Today any shipboard rumour is called a 'buzz', the term dating from the introduction of wireless into the Navy. Because of their involvement with communications, wireless ratings are usually the first to learn of matters affecting ships' movements, etc.

The Second World War brought an enormous increase in the Navy's personnel, and these 'Hostilities Only' ratings speedily absorbed and added to existing lower deck slang terms for food and drink. Thus sausages were dubbed 'bangers' – in the first world conflict, when served with mashed potatoes, they had been known as 'Zeppelins in a cloud' – eggs were either 'chicken fruit' or 'cackle berries'; bacon and baked beans (the latter a wartime innovation) a 'cowboy's breakfast'; pea soup became 'pea doo'; and any kind of suet pudding 'figgy duff', notwithstanding that these were generally made with anything but figs. Any extra piece of food, especially cheese, added to one's plate was called a 'jockey'; a second helping as 'going round the buoy'; and anything additional in the way of leftovers of food as 'gash'; e.g., 'any gash going?' The individual asking for this might well be dubbed a 'gannet' by his messmates,

Mealtime in a Lower Deck mess on board a modern British warship.

since it is well known that seagulls are insatiable. Any kind of soft drink obtained from the canteen was called a 'goffer', and chocolate purchased from the same source known as 'nutty', whether or not it actually contained nuts. 'Nutty', incidentally, became useful currency for barter or as a return for a favour granted, and was often used for such humanitarian purposes as a comfort for refugees or rescued survivors from torpedoed ships – even if the latter were enemy personnel.

Soon after the end of the Second World War, as part of promised improvements in amenities in the Fleet, centralised messing was gradually introduced in all new construction warships, along with self-service dining halls and electrically equipped galleys and serving rooms. These innovations, together with enormously improved culinary standards and other advances in catering management have resulted in the provision of gourmet-style meals in all naval ships and establishments, and a wide variety of dishes for the sailor to choose from on his daily menus. In consequence much of the picturesque slang of the past associated with food and messing has disappeared from the vocabulary of the British Navy man of today.

CHAPTER III

The Departed Spirit

Some of the wartime slang terms introduced by 'Hostilities Only' ratings applied also to the rum issue. In the pre-war Navy, and in fact stretching far back into the distant past, a rating's daily tot had always constituted a valuable item of barter to be offered in exchange for various favours from his shipmates, a practice severely frowned on by Authority. 'It may not be known to everyone that it is grog which pays all debts and not money in a man-of-war'.* Back in 1850 when the grog ration was ordered to be issued at mid-day only, the Admiralty decreed that 'all sale, loan, barter or transfer of grog' was strictly prohibited. The practice continued notwithstanding.

According to established lower deck etiquette, the tot as soon as drawn was handed over to the person granting the favour, who drank most of it, but was expected politely to hand back a token mouthful to be consumed, or 'seen off', by the donor. The 1939-45 wartime entries, however, instituted their own version of tot barter by actually stipulating the quantity of the liquor they were prepared to offer, categorising this as 'sippers' or 'gulpers' according to the worth of the favour granted. Thus the former term meant taking merely a sip of the proffered tot, the latter consuming it all. Regular Navy men regarded this variation of a long established practice with disgust.

Then, in 1970, a shattering blow was struck at British naval tradition when the sailor's daily rum ration was abolished. With it also went a number of long-standing customs.

As mentioned earlier, beer had for many years constituted an integral part of the sailor's official daily ration. But in the days of sailing warships two problems had to be overcome: that of finding enough room on board to stow the liquor, and its keeping qualities.

* *Nautical Economy, or Forecastle Recollections of Events during the last War*, Jack Nastyface, 1836.

Accordingly when ships were embarking stores prior to sailing, they were instructed to take on as much beer as they could conveniently stow, making up with wine and spirit. The former was usually Spanish red wine, and the latter brandy. The Admiralty decreed that when alternatives to beer became necessary, the men could have either a daily half pint of spirit or a pint of locally purchased wine in lieu. In the Mediterranean red wine was the usual tipple purchased for the ratings. But this was poor stuff, for the men dubbed it 'Black Strap', and to be sent to the Mediterranean was to be 'black-strapped'. If either could be obtained, the sailors preferred two cheap Spanish wines known as *Rosolio* and *Mistela*. The latter, a fiery white wine, was affectionately referred to as 'Miss Taylor'.

In 1655 when Jamaica was captured by Admiral Penn, rum soon began to supersede brandy. It was cheap, easy to obtain, and improved with keeping. The value of rum, especially on overseas stations, was gradually appreciated by those responsible for the Navy's victualling, and in 1731 it became an official issue to seamen, the daily half pint being issued in two equal parts, one in the morning and the other in the evening.

This innovation achieved rapid acceptance in the British Fleet. But in those days the spirit was issued neat, and drunkenness became so rife in the ships of the West Indies squadron that the Commander-in-Chief, Vice-Admiral Edward Vernon (struck off the list of flag officers in 1746 for treading on the corns of Authority), was appalled. Writing to the Admiralty in August 1740 he informed Their Lordships that:

> Observing that recent frequent desertions have principally arisen from men stupefying themselves with Spirituous Liquors, I have, after consulting my captains and surgeons, ventured to attack that formidable Dragon, Drunkenness, by giving the general order enclosed.

This read:

> To Captains of the Squadron! Whereas the Pernicious Custom of the Seamen drinking their Allowance of Rum in Drams, and often at once, is attended by many fatal Effects to their Morals as

well as their Health, the daily allowance of half a pint a man is to be mixed with a quart of water, to be mixed in one Scuttled Butt kept for that purpose, and to be done upon Deck, and in the presence of the Lieutenant of the Watch, who is to see that the men are not defrauded of their allowance of Rum; it is to be served in two servings, one in the morning and the other in the afternoon. The men that are good Husbands may from the savings of their Salt Provisions and Bread purchase Sugar and Limes to make the water more palatable to them. Dated 21 August 1740 on board HMS *Burford* in Port Royal Harbour.

The dilution henceforth became known as 'grog' because of the admiral's nickname of 'Old Grog', a reference to his habit of wearing clothing made of grogram. Some forty years later, Doctor Thomas Trotter, a surgeon on board HMS *Berwick* and an amateur rhymster, recorded the attachment of this appellation to the brew in the following lines:

> *A mighty bowl on deck he drew,*
> *And filled it to the brink;*
> *Such drank the* Burford's *gallant crew,*
> *And such the gods shall drink.*
> *The sacred robe which Vernon wore*
> *Was drenched within the same,*
> *And hence his virtues guard our shore,*
> *And Grog derives its name.*

After Trafalgar it also became known as 'Nelson's blood', since it was commonly believed on the lower deck that after his death the body of Lord Nelson was conveyed back to this country inside a barrel of neat rum to preserve it, and that the spirit was tapped by the sentries keeping watch over it. As shown by the following account by the surgeon of HMS *Victory*, however, the legend was false.

On the day after the battle there was no lead on board to make a coffin. A cask, called a *leaguer*, which is of the largest size on shipboard, was therefore chosen for the reception of the body which, after the hair had been cut off, was stripped of the clothes except the shirt and put into it, and the cask was then filled with brandy.

In the evening after this melancholy task was accomplished, the gale came on with violence from the south-west and continued that night and the succeeding day without any abatement. During this boisterous weather Lord Nelson's body remained under the charge of a Sentinel on the middle deck. The cask was placed on its end, having a closed aperture at its top and another below, the object of which was that as a frequent renewal of the spirit was thought necessary, the old could be drawn off below and the fresh quantity introduced above without moving the cask or occasioning the least agitation of the body.

On the 24th there was a disengagement of air from the body to such a degree that the sentry became alarmed on seeing the head of the cask raised; he therefore applied to the officers, who were under the necessity of having the cask spiled [holed] to give the air a discharge. After this no considerable collection of air took place. The spirit was drawn off once and the cask filled again before the arrival of the *Victory* at Gibraltar on the 28th, where spirit of wine was procured, and the cask showing a deficit by the body's absorbing a considerable quantity of the brandy, was then filled up with it. Brandy was used in the proportion of two-thirds to one of spirit of wine.*

With the daily allowance of rum remaining at half a pint per man there was still a good deal of drunkenness on board ship, which reached a peak during the French wars between 1790 and 1815. The admirals and captains on the spot saw the evil at first hand. Experience showed that the rum ration was a constant source of inefficiency in their ships and squadrons, and they were continually urging the Admiralty to reduce the spirit ration.

In 1812 Admiral Keith represented to Their Lordships:

It is observable and deeply to be lamented that almost every crime except theft originates in drunkenness ... it is an evil of great magnitude, and one it will be impossible to prevent so long as the present excessive quantity of spirits is issued in the Royal Navy. It is at all times a delicate point to interfere with what is

* *The Death of Lord Nelson*, Wm Beaty MD.

called an allowance or right, and the present may not be the moment for reforming even so great an evil; but in the event of peace I am satisfied that not a more essential service could be rendered to the nation than to reduce the quantity of spirits now used in the Navy.

Nevertheless the excessive rum issue was allowed to continue unchecked until well after the Battle of Waterloo. The allowance remained at two gills a day until 1823 when tea was added to the daily rations. By this time the demand for men to join the Navy had fallen spectacularly, and the numbers of volunteers for ordinary peacetime requirements were proving sufficient. In the following year the Admiralty took the plunge, cut the ration by half and discontinued the evening issue. But this reform was neutralised by the adoption of the Imperial measure in 1826, a change which added one-fifth to the rum ration, and the evening issue was resumed.

In an effort to curb drunkenness, 'drinking at the tub' was tried. This meant that instead of the grog being served out to the cooks of messes to be taken below to the men, the mess basins of the whole ship's company were laid out in rows beside the tub. The cook received the allowance for his messmates in the mess 'kit', a small oval wooden tub, and divided it into the basins. The men then came forward in line, and each picked up his basin and drank his grog, passing over the empty basin to the opposite side. It also became the custom at the same time to drink to the health of the Sovereign, each man doffing his hat as he did so. This practice was later commemorated by inscribing the loyal toast 'The King God Bless Him' in brass letters on the side of the rum tub, the wording being suitably altered on the accession of Queen Elizabeth II.

The grog remaining in the 'kit' after each man's allowance had been measured out was known as 'plushers', from the French *plus*. Strictly this should have been poured down the scupper along with any remaining in the rum tub, but once the ration had been taken below it was regarded as the rum cook's perks.

'Drinking at the tub' acted as an efficient check on drunkenness and found favour with ships' medical officers. But it was generally regarded as contrary to the habits of the Service, and, moreover, seriously interfered with the time allotted for dinner, since the rum issue in a large ship took as long as twenty-five minutes. It was not, therefore, generally adopted except as a mode of punishment.

In 1850 a committee was appointed to enquire into the subject of drunkenness in the Navy, witness after witness stating that the bulk of crimes and offences committed on board ship were attributable to the second 'tub'. The result was a recommendation to reduce the allowance by half, abolish the evening serving and give no allowance to cadets and boys. These recommendations were adopted, and the ration reduced to one-eighth of a pint, at which it remained until that historic day in 1970. Pay was increased in compensation, and men not wishing to take up their spirit ration could receive grog money in lieu based on the value of the spirit, or, alternatively, extra tea and sugar instead. In 1881 the issue of a rum ration to officers other than warrant officers ceased altogether, while in the case of the ship's company the issue was limited to men over the age of twenty.

On board ship the rum issue had become part of the official daily routine, and also something of a ceremony, which was still faithfully carried on to the day of its abolition. Thus every day at the pipe of 'Up Spirits' at six bells in the forenoon watch a small procession wound its way below to the spirit room. Leading the way was the 'Captain of the Hold', a seaman or marine traditionally known as 'Tanky' from his original connection with the old-time master who in sailing warships was responsible for the stowage of the hold, including the beer and fresh water casks. Accompanying him was a rating of the supply branch, nicknamed by tradition 'Jack Dusty'; a seaman petty officer, a regulating petty officer, and the Officer of the Day.

The ratings carried with them a small brass-bound *barrico*, or breaker. From a tapped cask the required quantity of neat spirit was drawn off and measured into the breaker, which was then padlocked and taken on deck. There the traditional wooden tub, successor to Admiral Vernon's 'scuttled butt', had been placed in readiness, together with an array of copper measures for mixing and serving out the grog.

After issuing the allowances due to the chief and petty officers, who were permitted to draw their tots neat, the rest of the spirit in the breaker was then emptied into the rum tub and the correct quantity of water added to make the 'two-water' mixture which in

Filling and sealing wicker-covered rum jars in the Royal Victoria Yard, Deptford for issue to small warships.

recent years had become the regular brew for lower ratings. Previously it had been 'three-water', or three parts of water to one of rum. The Officer of the Day then took up his supervisory position as of old 'to see that no man is defrauded of his proper allowance'. Precisely at noon, eight bells were struck, the bugler sounded the 'rum call', and issue commenced. In older times the ship's fiddlers played 'Nancy Dawson' or some other lively tune at eight bells as a signal that the grog was ready to be served out.

Although the Navy's rum was originally obtained from Jamaica, in more recent times it had become a blend of rums imported from Demerara, Trinidad and Barbados. Arriving in the victualling yards at 140 degrees over proof, it was gradually broken down by the addition of water until it had been reduced to a strength of 95.5 degrees under proof before being issued to ships and establishments at home and abroad.

In the old days proof was determined at the Royal Arsenal by mixing pure alcohol and water with grains of black gunpowder heated by the sun through a burning glass, which just allowed the gunpowder to ignite. The story goes that on board ship the purser used to have to carry out this test. If the rum was too strong he was killed by the explosion, and everyone could help themselves to the good mixture. If it was too weak and no ignition took place, the purser was hanged for watering down the sailors' rum. The Admiralty became so concerned with the increasing shortage of pursers that they adopted Sike's hydrometer, and this method of determining proof was used thereafter!

In the autumn of 1969 discussions within the Ministry of Defence as to the continuance or otherwise of the Navy's rum ration concluded that this time-hallowed tradition should now come to an end. In effect the Navy itself made the decision, because the number of rum-drinkers had steadily decreased over the years since the end of the Second World War. The tot had become an anachronism which in the modern Navy was suspect in relation to working efficiency; and the introduction of breath tests for civilian car drivers did not help supporters of the retention of the daily issue of grog. The sum of threepence a day paid to those who did not 'draw' was scarcely an incentive towards temperance, and the fading interest in this naval tradition was evidence not only of changing habits, but of a more responsible approach to work and career. This was a sum of the arguments, and Nelson's sailors would have turned in their graves at such heresy.

'Efficiency must be the arbiter of all activities within a fighting service', declaimed the Admiralty Board, 'and everything must be mercilessly scrutinised to this end. After his mid-day rum issue doubt must lie on a sailor's ability to handle the intricate weapons and electrical systems of Britain's modern fighting ships. Too much is at stake to take that chance'.

Accordingly it was decreed that the issue of rum would be abolished with effect from 1st August 1970. 'I am not expecting to rocket to "Top of the Pops" in the Navy on this', the then First Sea Lord, the late Admiral Sir Michael Le Fanu, ruefully quipped to pressmen. But surprisingly enough, the decision was received by the Fleet with comparatively little protest, although the final issue of rum was made something of an occasion for mourning.

On 31st July on board the aircraft carrier *Albion* at Portsmouth, newspaper reporters and photographers representing the world's press looked on as ratings queued for the last time for their ration of 'Nelson's blood'. Chief Petty Officers in the Royal Naval Barracks gathered round a candle-lit 'altar' in their mess as the last tots were issued from a crepe-draped barrel standing in a coffin alongside a death mask. On board the cruiser *Belfast*, then an accommodation ship for the Reserve Fleet, the latter itself soon to be doomed to extinction, the traditional stirring of the 1½-cwt Christmas pudding was brought forward so that the mixture could be laced with four pints of Navy rum. At Portsmouth city's main post office a specially engraved commemorative cover was issued, letters being stamped 'Last Day of Issue Navy Rum 31 July 1970'.

In the missile destroyer HMS *Fife*, then on a visit to Pearl Harbour, Hawaii, the ceremony of the 'Funeral of the Tot' was recorded on American television. At the shore establishment of HMS *Jufair* in the Persian Gulf, a rum barrel with a headstone to mark 'the last resting place of a good and faithful servant' was ceremonially interred, the committal service, written and read by the establishment's chaplain who hoped it wasn't blasphemy, including the following:

> For as much as it hath pleased the Lord High Admirals to take away from us the issue of our dearly beloved tot, we therefore commit its cask to the ground, sip to sip, splashes to splashes, thirst to thirst, in the sure and certain knowledge that it will never again be restored to us; but with the glorious hope that it might be according to the mighty working whereby M.O.D. (Navy) is able to accomplish all things unto itself.

Two pipers from the resident military unit in Bahrein, the 2nd Battalion, Royal Irish Rangers, played a lament.

On board HMS *Dido*, at sea off the north-east coast of Scotland, the last tot was thrown overboard in a sealed bottle together with a note asking the finder to drink the Navy's health. HMS *Dolphin*, the submarine base at Gosport, paraded a gun carriage on which a coffin containing a sample of 'the departed spirit' was borne, led by a piper, flanked by drummers and followed by a guard of honour.

But there were to be compensations. 'The issue of rum is a particularly naval privilege of very long standing,' the Admiralty Board announced. 'Its abolition is not an economy measure. A capital sum of £2,700,000 will therefore be paid into a new Sailors' Fund, to be used solely for the benefit of ratings and Royal Marine other ranks, who will play a major part in the administration of this Fund'. Chief and petty officers were now to be allowed to buy spirits in their messes on board ship, a privilege previously enjoyed only by officers; and junior ratings could have an increased daily ration of tinned beer. Grog money, however, ceased to be paid as such, being absorbed into the 'military salary' which had been introduced to replace the old pay scales in all three services earlier in the year.

However rum has not disappeared from the Navy completely. The traditional order to 'Splice the Main Brace' is still made on special occasions. At such times each officer and rating over the age of eighteen is issued with one-eighth of a pint of spirits, or two 12-oz cans of beer if spirits are not available.

Although the meaning of this expression is well known, its origin is somewhat obscure. It has long been the custom in the Royal Navy for an extra issue of spirits to be made in exceptional circumstances, such as after a particularly arduous spell of service or strenuous job of work. In a sailing warship the main brace was one of the stoutest ropes in the running rigging. If during an action this had been shot away, or had parted in rough weather, and a spare was not available, the work of splicing it was a task of such difficulty and rarity that it merited an extra rum ration for those who carried out the work. It is in this connection that the expression, which is known to have been used in the early part of the eighteenth century, is said to have its origin. The regulations of the time stated in fact that 'extra issues of spirits are not to be made other than in very exceptional circumstances, such as occasions of particularly arduous service or exposure'.

Today the order to 'Splice the Main Brace' is only given to mark some special event, such as an official visit to the Fleet by the Sovereign, a Coronation, or the signing of an armistice at the successful conclusion of a long war. Some stocks of rum are also held in the naval victualling yards for supply to ships employed under arduous conditions, such as in Arctic waters. Rum in these ships is issued only at the discretion of the captain.

CHAPTER IV

The Social Side

From early times the crews of warships, then generally referred to as 'the people', divided themselves into messes of from four to eight members apiece. A 'mess' was the smallest sub-division of a ship's company for the purposes of eating and sleeping, and the word dates from the days of the first Queen Elizabeth, when the hands sat down in groups to 'mess from the common pot'. Incidentally, the generic term 'Lower Deck' to denote the non-commissioned ranks and ratings of the Royal Navy originated from the fact that in the old 'wooden walls' their messes were always situated on the lower gun deck.

Each mess was furnished with a long deal table, secured at one end to the ship's side and suspended from a rope or hook at the other, so that it could be hoisted up to the deckhead out of the way when not in use. For seating, two long wooden stools were provided; also a bread barge in which to stow the mess's daily allowance of hard tack, a small barrico for vinegar, and the 'kit' in which to draw the mess's grog ration or any other form of liquid refreshment.

Plates made of tinned wrought iron, basins of the same metal, or of wood, and individual tin 'hookpots',* were supplied as 'mess traps', but the only item of individual cutlery, or flatware, was a tinned wrought iron spoon for each man. In some ships the messes, spaced between the guns, were separated and shut off from each other by small screens of canvas for greater privacy. With the advent of ironclad warships, properly enclosed messes with suitable furniture were set aside for chief and petty officers. The mess was not only the place where the sailor ate his meals; it was also where he slung his hammock and kept his few personal belongings.

This general form of mess-deck layout, known as 'broadside

---

* Today the 'hookpot' still exists only as a naval slang term, usually applied to a ship in a derogatory sense, as, for example: 'I'm fed up with this bloody hookpot!'

Messdeck scene in the old Navy. Note the hanging mess table and wooden 'kit'.

Chief Petty Officers' mess in a guided missile destroyer.

messing', with various refinements added over the years in the way of furniture and crockery as lower deck living conditions were improved, remained the standard in most warships of the British Navy up to, and even beyond, the Second World War. Larger vessels coming into service prior to 1939, such as aircraft carriers, were, however, provided with special recreation spaces in which the men could foregather in off-duty hours. Padded armchairs, cushioned benches and writing desks were other lower deck amenities provided.

In the old sailing warships officers' messes were also little short of primitive. Starting literally at the lower end of the scale was the midshipmen's berth. A first-rate usually carried twenty-four of these 'young gentlemen', some of whom went to sea at as early an age as eleven, with a proportionate number in lesser rates. They messed in the after cockpit on the orlop deck, a non-fighting deck immediately above the hold, which all contemporary accounts agree was not a pleasant place.

The berth was in fact a dingy den, into which faint daylight was admitted through a thick, dirt-encrusted glass scuttle let into the ship's side. In size the compartment was usually about twelve feet square and five feet four inches high, so that for some it was impossible to stand upright. The atmosphere was foul, the prevailing odours being compounded of bilgewater, old rope, gin, beer and frying onions. Most of the space was taken up by a deal table covered with a cloth or an old hammock which had to last a week, heavily stained and spotted since it was frequently utilised by the occupants on which to clean their knives and forks. Lighting was provided by lanterns and 'purser's glims', tallow candles stuck in tin sconces. Sea chests were used for seats, and there were wooden lockers in which to stow items of food, bread, table utensils, etc. In action the after cockpit became the surgeon's operating theatre, when it was littered with knives, saws, tourniquets, sponges, basins and water, the table and chests then being used for amputations and other crude forms of surgery for the wounded.

As well as the midshipmen, the berth was also the home of the master's mates, the captain's clerk and the surgeon's mates. The food was the same as that provided for the men, supplemented with items obtained by the mess caterer, usually a senior master's mate. Each member paid him between £3 and £5 on joining, and about £1 a month while the ship was in commission. Before leaving England the caterer laid in a supply of potatoes and onions, the former being stowed in the lockers and the latter hung from the deck beams. Dutch cheeses, tea and coffee, pepper and sugar were also among his purchases. In harbour he bought 'soft tommy' (bread) and boxes of red herrings.

The mess was divided informally into 'oldsters' and 'youngsters', the former sometimes including men aged forty and over who had long qualified for and were still awaiting promotion. It was governed partly by strong-arm methods and partly by certain laws. 'Speaking of the midshipmen's berth and of the occasional ruggedness of manners, I shall be doing wrong to leave an impression that they were a mere lawless set of harum-scarum scamps. Quite the contrary, for we had a code of laws for our government which, for precision and directness of purpose, might have rivalled many of those promulgated by the newest born states of the world'.* Thus any member caught eating, or drinking rum, on the day he had been invited to dine in the lieutenants' mess or the captain's cabin was sentenced to be 'firked' or 'cobbed'. This unofficial flogging was administered with a stockingful of sand, a knotted rope or the bung stave of a cask.

When the evening issue of grog began to flow in the mess, and the conversation became 'neither prudish nor refined' and was thus considered unfit for the ears of the youngsters, the senior member would stick a fork into one of the overhead deck beams. This was a sign that these youths must leave the mess immediately and retire to their hammocks. Anyone who disregarded the signal, or was slow to obey, was 'firked' with a knotted rope. When ironclad warships finally ousted the 'wooden walls' and the appropriate action became physically impossible, the mess president merely had to utter the words 'Fork in the beam' for the younger members instantly to make themselves scarce on pain of condign punishment.

As time went on this traditional custom, which lasted well into recent times, was supplemented by newer rules. Thus the cry of 'Breadcrumbs!' required all younger members of the mess to stop their ears; 'Fishbones!' meant that they were to close their eyes; and 'Matchboxes!' that they were to shut their mouths and

* *Fragments of Voyages and Travels*, Captain Basil Hall RN, 1832.

maintain strict silence. Slackness in obeying, or outright disobedience, was rewarded with some *ad hoc* form of punishment, which frequently bordered on the sadistic, dreamed up and ordered by the mess president.

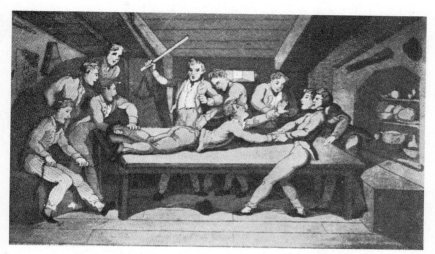

An offender being 'cobbed' in the midshipmen's berth.

Other customs practised in the midshipmen's berth, some of which lingered on into the twentieth century Navy, included the ceremony of 'christening' a newly appointed midshipman. This involved breaking a plate or a ship's biscuit over the head of the victim, who was also required to drink a glass of seawater. In addition he was frequently given a dozen strokes on the backside with his own dirk scabbard for having the temerity to bring his name to sea!

It was not unknown for the victim to have a broad arrow lightly nicked on his nose with a razor, the owner of the nose to heal the soonest being subsequently dealt with again in order to chasten his vile body for so soon discarding His Majesty's mark.*

'Snotty' has for years been the slang term for a midshipman. It derives from the allegation that the 'young gentlemen' used to make their sleeves do duty as a handkerchief, and that to discourage this

* *A Few Naval Customs, Expressions, Traditions & Superstitions*, Beckett, 1931.

practice, buttons were placed on their cuffs. Junior midshipmen were always known as 'warts' or 'crabs', and no opportunity was ever lost of impressing upon them their lowly status. This treatment included the infliction of crude practical jokes, such as tying a 'slippery hitch' in a youngster's hammock lanyard, so that it would unexpectedly let him down when he attempted to board it; stowing a round shot under his blankets, or even cutting him down as he slept. Other tricks practised on the young innocent included hiding his trousers in the galley oven; sending him up on deck to 'hear the dogfish bark', or to ask the marine half deck sentry for the 'key of the keelson'; even making him drunk on rum and sending him up to the officer of the watch with a spoof message.

The sons of royalty sent afloat were apt to fare as badly as any of their socially inferior contemporaries. But when the young Prince William, son of George III, joined his first ship as a midshipman in 1779, one tough youngster greeted his arrival in the mess by demanding aggressively to know, 'By what name are you rated in the ship's books?'

'I am entered as Prince William Henry,' the newcomer replied cheerfully, 'but my father's name is Guelph, and therefore if you please you may call me William Guelph, for I am nothing more than a sailor like yourselves'.

This disarming reply earned him the grudging respect of his messmates, and, since he showed himself to be very ready to give as good as he got, he was not subjected to any special indignities.

Such was not the case, however, with the late King George V when a cadet in the training ship *Britannia*. In later life the king recalled ruefully, 'It never did me any good to be a prince, I can tell you, and many was the time I wished I hadn't been.' The late Duke of Windsor and his brother King George VI, who both served in the Navy, were compelled to suffer equally painfully at the hands of youthful tormentors when training as cadet and midshipman.

In the days of sailing warships the Gunner was responsible for the instruction of the junior officers, and the younger members of the midshipmen's berth were required to sling their hammocks in his quarters, known as the 'gunroom', which was situated in the after part of the lower gun deck, next above the orlop deck. In early printed orders respecting the duties of this officer appears the following instruction:

He is to keep order in the gunroom and suffer none to lie there but such as have a right thereto by their places or when the captain shall direct. He is to cause a careful man of his crew to watch there every night with a candle in a lantern.

The latter was frequently dubbed by his young charges the 'lady of the gunroom', although this title was more truly applicable to the wretched youth who cooked for the 'young gentlemen', washed up and cleaned out the midshipmen's berth. Applied to the later gunroom mess steward of more recent times, this term, too, lasted well into the present day.

Oddly enough, it was the more senior of a warship's officers, such as the lieutenants and marine officers, the chaplain, surgeon, master and the purser, who at first lacked a mess of their own; generally taking their meals in their sleeping quarters or cabins. These were individual spaces, usually on the middle deck, partitioned off by light wood or canvas bulkheads, which could be taken down and stowed below with their furniture in action.

In larger vessels, however, there was, situated immediately beneath the principal, or 'great cabin', which was reserved for the captain or admiral, a store room for valuables known as the 'Ward Robe'. About the middle of the eighteenth century the lieutenants and their professional brethren began to use this compartment for meals in preference to eating in their own cabins, and soon it came to be known as the 'Lieutenants' Mess'. But in inferior rates they used the gunroom, the subordinate officers continuing to mess in the midshipmen's berth.

In 1856 the whole position was regularised by the Admiralty. The 'Lieutenants' Mess' officially became the 'Wardroom', and the junior officers' mess, which included the midshipmen, the 'Gunroom'.

The captain, of course, lived alone, taking his meals by himself, except when he unbent sufficiently to invite some of the other officers to his table. His cabin, divided into separate sleeping and living quarters, was traditionally known as the 'Cuddy', and this term is still in use today. According to *The British Mariner's Vocabulary* by Doctor J.J. Moore, in olden times the 'cuddy' was a sort of cook room or cabin near the stern. In some ships the captain, if he had private means, lived in truly grand style.

The wardroom in a Victorian man-of-war. Note the coal stove, and officer of the watch in frock coat with telescope.

The next moment he stood in the presence of the captain, who was reclining on a sofa in the after cabin, where was blended a strange medley of rough tokens of war with the softer attributes of peace; here ranged well-filled bookcases – there double-barrelled pistols, and Turkish and French sabres. Here polished mahogany satin chairs, vases of flowers and billet-deux – there stern cold iron in the shape of 18-pounders taking their way through the ports hung with silk curtains – their icy touch and strained lashings told their scorn of the painter's art to render them less ferocious, in white and green – in the fore cabin hung a beautiful ormolu lamp over a festive board, where, when at sea, smoked eight silver covers at least (every day at 4 p.m.) with all the delicacies of the world – now garnished with a fine green cloth, cut-glass decanters, different sorts of wine, and a luncheon on a tray, after the most approved modes of the fashionable world. In short, all was of the most refined elegance, of the most approved taste, of the most exquisite delicacy, and of the richest description, side by side with the instruments of stern and instant destruction. In five minutes all would disappear, and the dogs let slip, fire, smoke, cartridges, bleeding bodies, recoiled guns; and fifty devils incarnate would turn this floating paradise to a hellish pandemonium!*

Nowadays the captain of a British warship lives in nothing like such style. He is always made an honorary member of the wardroom mess, although he would never dream of entering it unless specifically invited.

In the modern Royal Navy gunrooms have become a thing of the past. The rank of cadet has been abolished, and all junior officers now join naval ships and shore establishments as full members of the wardroom mess. Here they may encounter the survivors of a number of interesting customs and traditions which have come down through the centuries. Not least of these have to do with drinking.

As we have seen, wine and spirits were from early times carried afloat since they formed part of the rations of both sailors and officers, and also partly as a substitute for water. Wine has another association with the sea in that both displacement and the carrying

* *The Navy at Home*, William Marsh, 1831.

capacity of a ship were measured in tons. For in olden times the
word 'ton' was spelt 'tun', and in those days a ship's carrying
capacity was gauged by the number of tuns of wine or other liquor
she could stow on board.

For many years, under certain well established but ill-defined
procedures, naval officers were allowed to ship large quantities of
wines and spirits free of duty. Under the Customs Consolidation
Act of 1876 which codified these allowances, admirals, for example,
were permitted no less than 1260 gallons of duty-free wine per
annum. This works out at something like 270 average sized glasses
per day! Lieutenants, on the other hand, if they were fortunate
enough to command their own ships, were entitled to a total of 105
gallons a year, or about a couple of dozen glasses a day.

Not all grades of flag officer, however, were entitled to ship as
much as 1260 gallons of their favourite tipple duty free. Vice-
admirals were restricted to 1050 gallons annually, and rear-
admirals 840. Captains in command of first-rates were entitled to
630 gallons, while their colleagues in second-rates could enjoy a
maximum of 420 gallons. Captains unlucky enough to be appointed
to inferior rates had to make do with just twice the amount
permitted to lieutenants in command.

If all this wine had actually been drunk by the Royal Navy's
admirals and captains, since it was intended exclusively for use on
board, it might well be wondered how Britannia managed to rule
the waves for so long. But in fact, although there were undoubtedly
some doughty drinkers serving afloat in the roistering days of the
past,* these generous allowances of duty-free wines were by no
means meant to be consumed in their entirety by flag and
commanding officers. Both then and now they had a certain
amount of official entertaining to conduct on board. For this
important aspect of their social duties an annual monetary
'entertaining allowance', designed to cover the cost of food and
drink for guests, has long been provided. (Flag officers also receive
'Table Money' at a rate fixed by the Ministry of Defence (Navy) for
the upkeep of their special messes.)

The quantities of duty-free spirits permitted were also generous.

---

* In the 1890s more officers were court-martialled in the Royal Navy for
drunkenness than for any other offence. But Army officers' messes normally
carried vast amounts of champagne around with them on campaigns.

Thus as late as 1911 flag officers were allowed three pints a day; captains and commanders-in-command one pint daily; lieutenants in command, and each wardroom and gunroom officer permitted to have spirits, one-third of a pint a day. These amounts, according to the official order, were not to represent personal consumption, but to provide a sufficient allowance for individual officers and guests. The quantity of wine allowed was to be reduced *pro rata*.

Besides this, officers, including admirals, also received an official rum ration daily. This was reduced by half in 1850 without financial compensation, and, as mentioned earlier on, the flag and wardroom officers' rum ration ceased altogether in 1881. Thereafter the only occasion on which naval officers became entitled to an official issue of rum was when the order to 'Splice the Main Brace' was given.

In 1951 the quantities of privileged wine and spirits formerly allowed to officers of the Royal Navy were swept away when naval duty-free privileges were overhauled and put on a footing 'more suitable to modern needs'. The regulations now in force permit of nothing remotely resembling the old-time concessions.

Most of the wardroom mess customs still observed in the Navy today have become hallowed by long tradition. Thus when the wine – usually port – is passed at dinner the decanters are always stoppered before the loyal toast is drunk. The custom implies that it is solely for this purpose that the wine is provided, and that it is no longer required after all have filled their glasses. But after the toast has been drunk, should the wine be passed around again, those who did not drink the loyal toast cannot partake. If by some extraordinary, and unthinkable, quirk of circumstance the mess is composed entirely of teetotallers except for the mess president, which means that there is only one person to drink the Sovereign's health, he is entitled to a glass of port at mess expense so that his messmates may give proof of their loyal sentiments.

Despite the publicity given to the Royal Navy today, it may not be generally known that the Senior Service enjoys the unique privilege of remaining seated to drink the health of the Sovereign. There are four possible origins for this cherished privilege. One is that when, in 1660, Charles II was about to take passage back to this country and his throne from Holland in HMS *Naseby*, he bumped his head on the overhead deck beams when rising to reply to a toast. Before setting out on this triumphal voyage a grand dinner was given on board the *Naseby* at which, incidentally, the ships of the squadron which had come to fetch the king were renamed, the *Naseby* becoming the *Royal Charles*.

Another theory is that William IV while Duke of Clarence, when dining on board a man-of-war, also bumped his head on a deck beam when he stood up. Yet a third school of thought believes that when George IV while Prince Regent was dining on board a warship, he exclaimed as the officers rose to drink the king's health, 'Gentlemen, pray be seated. Your loyalty is above suspicion'. Since the Prince Regent was continually at variance with his father over political matters and was closely associated with the Parliamentary Opposition to the king, it is a matter for speculation as to whom their loyalty was directed. For in the Navy generally, loyalty to the person of the Sovereign took precedence over the ties of service to a political party.

It is true that in most of the old-time warships it was practically impossible to stand upright between decks except right amidships; and as most vessels of that era had a 'tumble-home' (i.e., the ship's side timbers curved inwards above the waterline), anyone seated close to the side would find it impossible to stand at all. Indeed, Captain Pellew, one of Nelson's 'band of brothers', complained in one ship he commanded that the 'tween deck space was so low, his servant had to dress his hair through the skylight.

Charles II might well have bumped his head, but that William IV should have been so clumsy seems doubtful, for he had been a sailor for years and was used to the peculiar inboard shape of ships. While a serving naval officer in the West Indies he had in fact acted as best man at the wedding of Captain Horatio Nelson, then commanding the frigate *Boreas*, to the attractive widow, Mrs Nisbet.

The fourth theory is that the custom originated in the Restoration Navy among gentleman volunteers, who formed the first considerable mess on board ship before the wardroom mess existed. Not being seamen by upbringing, they are likely to have found it difficult to keep their feet in a seaway. It was one of them who wrote:

> *Our paper, pen and ink, and we*
> *Roll up and down our ships at sea.*

In Charles II's time there was one more outburst of volunteering in the Elizabethan sense. And it was quite a big outburst because the Fleet was large and the consequent demand numerically great. The Second and Third Dutch Wars witnessed a veritable craze among the *jeunesse dorée* of the Restoration Court to take part in the rough-and-tumble of a sea-fight. Young bloods crowded into the ships to serve, if only for one campaign, under such distinguished patrons as the Dukes of York and Albemarle, and Prince Rupert. The very name 'volunteer' had a new lease of life. But they were not quite of the calibre of the Elizabethan voluntary gentlemen: they were too dilettante, too much the 'fair weather' sailors. At least, so thought Mr Samuel Pepys, and as soon as he had his way he dropped something like a guillotine upon them.*

In 1964, on the occasion of the Tercentenary of the Corps, the privilege of drinking the loyal toast seated was granted by Queen Elizabeth II to officers and non-commissioned officers of the Royal Marines. Two years later the Queen extended the privilege to chief and petty officers of the Royal Navy when dining formally in their messes, both ashore and afloat.

Whatever the truth of its origin, this particular naval custom goes by the board if the National Anthem should be played while the loyal toast is being drunk when the Queen, the Duke of Edinburgh, or any other member of the Royal Family is present. For then all naval and marine officers, ratings and other ranks, must stand like everyone else – unless the Royal Personage has expressed the wish that they should remain seated. Officers who serve in the Royal Yacht *Britannia*, however, make a practice of standing when drinking the loyal toast. They do this to emphasise the honoured distinction of serving in a royal yacht.

Soon after Britain's last battleship, HMS *Vanguard*, was commissioned for service in 1947 she was presented with the silver and ebony snuffbox which had once belonged to Captain Hardy of Trafalgar fame. The latter had commanded the fifth *Vanguard* which was Nelson's flagship at the Battle of the Nile, and he was with Nelson when the admiral died in the cockpit of the *Victory*

---

* *The Navy of Britain*, Lewis.

seven years later. The firm which had originally sold Hardy his snuff managed to provide a supply of the same kind that he had used, and each night in the battleship's wardroom Hardy's snuffbox was passed round after the loyal toast.

In former days in naval officers' messes there was a special toast for every night in the week, which was drunk after the loyal toast. They were as follows:

Monday night	– 'Our ships at sea'
Tuesday night	– 'Our native land'
Wednesday night	– 'Ourselves and no one like us'
Thursday night	– 'A bloody war or a sickly season'
Friday night	– 'A willing foe and sea room'
Saturday night	– 'Sweethearts and wives'
Sunday night	– 'Absent friends'

In the days when promotion was by seniority only and largely a matter of stepping into dead men's shoes, Thursday night's toast meant of course that in either of the contingencies named, opportunities for advancement would be greatly accelerated. Thus the toast was sometimes worded: 'A bloody war and quick promotion'.

In most wardroom messes today only the Saturday night toast is honoured. It is often the custom for the mess president to call upon the youngest officer present to reply for the ladies, and many a clever and witty speech is heard on these occasions.

Any officer who mentions a lady's name at dinner in a wardroom mess can be fined a round of port. But the president may make an exception if the lady happens to be well known or celebrated, say, a film star or perhaps a woman politician. This is done because all conversation at the table is considered public, and it is bad form to speak of a lady publicly. For the same reason any officer speaking in a foreign language at the dinner table, other than of course quoting the odd tag of dog Latin, may at the mess president's discretion be fined a round of port. Conversation being public should be conducted in a language understood by all. Any officer making a bet at the dinner table renders himself liable to the fine of a round of port, this custom having originally been instituted so that argument should not become heated nor give reason for a quarrel.

It is considered very bad manners to enter a strange mess

wearing a sword. The reason behind this was that any aggrieved party was thus prevented from arriving on board with the express intention of forcing a quarrel. Also no officer may draw a sword in the mess without previously asking permission, on pain of buying drinks all round. The origin of this custom was to prevent any hasty action when tempers ran high, particularly in the days when duelling was prevalent. In fact, an official ban on duelling continued to be included in the King's Regulations and Admiralty Instructions up until 1936. The relevant Article began with the words: 'Every officer in his Majesty's Fleet is hereby ordered neither to send nor to accept a challenge to fight a duel'.

Occasionally a wardroom mess president may lay himself open to a charge of transgressing the rules it is his duty to administer, and must thereby suffer appropriate punishment. Thus if he should leave the table at the conclusion of dinner and absent-mindedly omit to have the wine decanters removed, his seat may be taken by any other officer present, who can pass the wine round – to be paid for by the president!

On guest nights if a Royal Marine band is in attendance, it is the custom for the mess president to invite the bandmaster into the mess to have a drink. A chair is provided for him to the president's right, and the bandmaster's glass filled by giving him a 'backhander'. This means placing the glass at the left of the decanter to be filled. By doing so the port does not have to be passed anti-clockwise. For when the decanters are placed on the mess table after the last course has been cleared away, they must always be passed from right to left.

It is considered bad manners when asking for food to be passed along the table to help oneself without first taking the dish or plate from the person passing it. No member may leave the table without first seeking permission from the president. Equally, anyone arriving late must also first ask the president's permission to be seated. Unless he has been detained on duty, he must forego any of the courses already served. Nor may any member of the mess receive or read a message brought in during dinner without first asking permission. And if any member should light up before the president has announced: 'Gentlemen, you may smoke', he renders himself liable to the customary fine of a round of drinks. Should a guest offend any of these rules, he may be warned or fined, and if the latter, his host will have to pay.

Along with these traditional mess customs certain slang terms connected with drinking are still current today. Thus, while in ancient times a 'long ship' was a vessel rowed by the Vikings, the term has become wardroom slang, although seldom heard, one hopes. For a 'long ship' signifies a vessel lacking in the Navy's traditional hospitality. Put more bluntly, that her officers permit a long time to elapse between drinks.

In contrast to this implied parsimony, it is always possible in the wardrooms of HM ships and establishments to 'celebrate the siege of Gibraltar', for this remark is used as an excuse to offer a guest a drink. The various sieges of the famous Rock – some fourteen in all – covered such a lengthy period of time that one could celebrate the affair on any day of the year. It is, however, a convention afloat that one does not drink in a naval wardroom until 'the sun is over the foreyard'. In sailing warship days, when the sun had reached that altitude the morning was considered sufficiently advanced to take a 'nooner'.

Sailors are somewhat less superstitious today than were their forebears afloat. But it is still possible for a visitor to a naval wardroom to earn himself a black look if he allows an empty glass to ring. For thus, it is said, he has sounded the knell of some unfortunate sailor who will die by drowning. But if the offender quickly reaches out and stops the glass from ringing he can breathe more easily. For now, as the old superstition has it, 'the Devil will take two soldiers instead'.

These customs and traditions are, in the main, observed as faithfully in the wardroom messes of naval shore establishments as they are on board actual warships, since the former are considered just as much 'ships' as those that float and fight.

CHAPTER V

'Stone Frigates'

In the days of the press-gangs there were no naval shore establishments for the accommodation of newly entered sailors, nor was there any form of pre-sea or technical training for them. As already mentioned, at each of the three 'home ports' of Chatham, Portsmouth and Devonport – the latter known until 1824 simply as 'Dock' by the snooty citizens of its near neighbour, Plymouth – there were moored a number of receiving ships, on board which the Navy's new entries, pressed men and volunteers alike, were roughly crammed until required to commission seagoing ships of the Fleet.

These vessels were usually little more than the decaying and insanitary hulks of once fine warships, frequently captured prizes, commanded by ageing officers physically unfit for active sea service. In 1820 after the end of the Napoleonic wars there were still in existence at Portsmouth, Devonport, Chatham and Sheerness seventeen of these receiving ships, ranging from former first-rates to sloops. One was moored in the London dock area, and another, a former French 32-gun vessel, at Deptford, once a busy building yard for the Navy and now the site of its largest victualling depot; there was even one in Cork harbour for the reception of Irish entries.

Despite the recommendation of the committee on naval manning in 1853 that shore accommodation should be provided, and a permanent reserve of men kept ready in the home ports to complete crews of ships not in commission, it was not until the closing years of the century that the construction of barracks was started. They were speedily christened 'stone frigates' by their inmates, a term still in use today.

The first of these establishments was built, not at Portsmouth as might have been expected in view of that port's long association with the Navy, but at Devonport in 1879. By now the latter boasted the busiest of naval building yards, having triumphantly survived its earlier rivalry with Plymouth, whose civic fathers had at one time even refused to supply fresh water to their up and coming neighbour in a feud in which the celebrated Doctor Johnson took sides. 'No, no', he had exclaimed during a visit to the city at the height of the affair, 'I am against the Dockers. I am a Plymouth man. Rogues! Let them die of thirst. They shall not have a drop.'

Portsmouth was, however, the next to have a naval barracks, construction of which was begun in 1899. Covering an area of $62\frac{1}{2}$ acres, the buildings were ready in the autumn of 1903, when four thousand seamen, stokers and marines left the hulks and marched out of the dockyard to take over their new home. Reported the *Hampshire Telegraph*:

> Taking possession of the new Naval Barracks by the Seamen, Marines and Stokers of the Portsmouth Naval Depot on Wednesday had something like the appearance of a triumphal procession. Immense crowds lined the route from the Dockyard to the main gates in Edinburgh Road, and the Bluejackets were cheered loudly as they passed along.
>
> The hulks were vacated with no ceremony or regret as they were unpleasant and miserable quarters. There had been two rehearsals for the 4,000 men of taking possession of the Barracks. All furniture and mess traps had been got in previously. On Wednesday there was no drill on the Depot Ground, all hands clearing up. After dinner the men mustered in four companies – Chief Petty Officers, Seamen, Stokers and Marines. There were four bands present from the Naval Barracks, HMS *Excellent*, HMS *St Vincent* and the Marines. At half past two the bugle sounded to go and the men marched off. There were immense crowds of spectators and difficulty was experienced by the Mounted Borough Police in keeping the road clear. Once inside, the gates were shut and the crowd besieged the railings to see what was to follow. The men were formed in a huge hollow square. Commander Stileman gave a few orders and closed with an intimation that there would be general leave that evening, an announcement which called forth a cheer. Then to some lively tunes the men marched off to their quarters.

Three months later, by command of King Edward VII, the men put

A modern 'stone frigate'. Aerial view of the R.N. Engineering College, Manadon, H.M.S. *Thunderer*.

up HMS *Victory* cap ribbons, although until 1st April 1905 all continued to be borne on the books of HMS *Firequeen*, at that time the yacht of the Commander-in-Chief, Admiral Sir John Fisher.

The reason why the king wanted the sailors in the naval barracks to wear *Victory* cap ribbons was that Nelson's old flagship was slowly decaying at her moorings in the harbour, and as the Admiralty had no plans to save her it seemed that her name would soon disappear from the Navy List. Furthermore, she had recently been severely damaged in a collision with the old battleship *Neptune*, which broke adrift while being towed out of Portsmouth harbour to be scrapped, and struck the *Victory* well below the waterline.

In imminent danger of sinking, the latter was hauled into dock in the nick of time. Even after being repaired, however, she continued to leak badly because of her rotten timbers. Then, in 1922, it was decided to place her in Number Two dock, restore her to her Trafalgar condition, and use her as a national memorial to Nelson and the Navy, the cost to be met by public subscription. This was done, and ever since she has acted as the flagship of successive Commanders-in-Chief.

In 1974 Queen Elizabeth II decreed that the ship name of the

barracks should be changed to HMS *Nelson* to avoid confusion
between the shore establishment and the admiral's old flagship.
The Royal Naval Barracks at Devonport had also undergone a
change of ship name. Originally HMS *Vivid*, this was later altered
to the name of another famous British sailor, Drake.

An interesting, if unhappy, item of history attaches to the naval
barracks at Portsmouth. Three years after the establishment was
opened, the railings round the barracks area were suddenly
reinforced with corrugated iron sheeting, thus effectively concealing
the activities of its inmates on the parade ground from the
interested gaze of passers-by in neighbouring Edinburgh Road.
The sheeting, known locally as 'Pompey's shame', was to remain in
position for many years, a reminder to those with long memories of
a near mutiny which occurred in the barracks in the winter of 1906.

The cause of the disturbances was a tactless command to go
down on their knees given by a young gunnery lieutenant to an
assembly of discontented stoker ratings so that he could speak
severely to them after they had noisily dispersed from a muster on
the parade ground in pouring rain. The lieutenant later maintained
that this, unofficial, 'on the knee' order had no derogatory meaning
and was in general use at the Gunnery School of HMS *Excellent*
when addressing a body of sailors. But it further inflamed the
tempers of the disgruntled stokers, whose resentment overflowed
later that evening into riots inside and outside the barracks
canteen. At the height of the uproar, mounted police were called
out to control the sizeable crowd of civilians and sailors who
gathered in Edinburgh Road, some of whom showed their
sympathy by joining the rioting stokers in hurling missiles. After
the Commodore himself had calmed the men down, the rest of the
night passed peacefully. But trouble broke out again on the
following evening and was only quelled with difficulty.

After order had finally been restored and a naval court of inquiry
had considered the affair, a series of courts-martial were held, a
number of alleged ringleaders of the riots being convicted on
charges of mutinous behaviour and sentenced to various terms of
imprisonment and dismissal from the Service. Finally the
lieutenant himself was court-martialled for improper use of the 'on
the knee' order and given a reprimand. It was to prevent any such
lamentable affair which might occur in the future from being

exposed to the public gaze that the iron sheeting was erected. Not until Commodore Thompson in 1956 obtained the Commander-in-Chief's permission for its removal was it finally taken down. 'Nothing occurs on the parade ground of which I have cause to be ashamed,' he wrote, 'and there is plenty going on of which I am proud'.

The Portsmouth naval riots of 1906 had a number of repercussions. The then commodore and two of his commanders were relieved of their appointments. There was a fierce debate in Parliament over the justice of the court martial findings. Most curious perhaps was the case of Edgar Wallace, the detective-story writer, then a star reporter for the *Daily Mail*, and one of the pressmen sent down from London to cover the affair. Because of the injudicious nature of the latter's stories, the lieutenant subsequently sued the newspaper for libel and succeeded in obtaining substantial damages out of court. As the result of a second, although unrelated, libel case brought against the newspaper soon afterwards, which had also been brought about by Wallace's careless reporting, the *Daily Mail* had to pay out the largest sum in damages which up to then had ever been awarded. Their star reporter was then fired!

In 1928, more than twenty years after the Portsmouth troubles, the lieutenant who had sparked them off, now a flag officer serving in the Mediterranean Fleet, became the flashpoint of another naval *cause célèbre* which arose from an unfortunate remark concerning the parentage of his flagship's marine bandmaster at a ship's dance. The captain and commander of the battleship in which the incident occurred who disliked the admiral and had complained to higher authority in a manner 'prejudicial to naval discipline', were court-martialled in a blaze of world publicity fanned by the press, and reprimanded. The admiral himself was summarily placed on the retired list. Because of what was regarded by an embarrassed Admiralty as his inept handling of the whole affair, the then Commander-in-Chief of the Mediterranean Fleet never realised his ambition to become First Sea Lord.

The third naval barracks was opened at Chatham, also in the year 1903, on the site of an old prison close to the naval dockyard, the basin and graving docks of which had been dug out by the prison inmates. The establishment was designated HMS *Pembroke* after the eighth ship of that name, previously HMS *Duncan*, an old 74-gun second-rate which had been the general depot ship at that port. Like the other newly opened 'stone frigates', hammock hooks were grouted into the walls of the men's living blocks, or 'mess decks', all of which bore the names of famous British sailors of the past; slinging rails installed between the roof support stanchions; and their floors fashioned from the teak deck planking of scrapped 'wooden walls'.

In 1872 all naval ratings were for the first time allotted official numbers. The Admiralty Order which introduced the system also brought into use the pay ledger on board ships to replace the old-time Muster Book. With the opening of the new barracks, from which in future ships of the Fleet would be manned, an initial letter was now added to each rating's official number to indicate the port to which he was to be returned when his ship paid off.

Thus the letter 'P' for Portsmouth; 'C' for Chatham; and 'D' for Devonport, according to his allocation to one or other of these three home ports, prefixed every man's official number. A further alphabetical letter was subsequently added to denote the branch of the Service to which he belonged. Four letters were chosen, more or less arbitrarily for this purpose: 'J' for all seamen ratings; 'K' for stokers; 'L' for stewards – then called 'Domestics' – and 'M' for artisans, artificers, writers, cooks, sick berth and stores ratings.

It was at his Port Division that a man's Service record was maintained throughout his naval career, unless he obtained permission to change it, and where he served when not at sea or under training. Furthermore, he could only be drafted to ships and shore bases which were manned from his home port by the latter's own drafting organisation. But during the Second World War it was found difficult to adhere to this system, and in 1957 a new centralised drafting organisation for the Navy was created, under which men would be able to select a depot for family welfare and holding purposes, and by a system of 'preference drafting' record their choice of the area in which they wished to serve when their turn came round for home service.

In due course each home port and its depot acquired its own special nickname, which have long become familiar to generations of sailors. Thus Portsmouth is known as 'Pompey'; Devonport as 'Guzz'; and Chatham as 'Chats'. From time to time nautical etymologists have endeavoured to trace the origins of these nicknames, but with the exception of 'Guzz' the results are unconvincing.

'Pompey', maintains one school of thought, dates back as far only to the lifetime of the Navy's former 'Friend', Dame Agnes Weston (1840-1918) who in 1876 founded the first 'Sailors' Rest' at Devonport. Known as 'Salvation Agnes', temperance meetings were her speciality, and in 1872 she launched a campaign in that port to combat the hard-drinking tendencies of the sailors. Designed to get the men off the streets and out of the pubs, the facilities she provided at her 'Rest' included meals, baths, lodging, recreation rooms and lounges. Religious services, temperance lectures and Bible readings were regularly held, but none of her customers was under any obligation to attend these gatherings. 'Aggie's' became so popular that in 1881 Miss Weston opened a second Sailors' Rest in Portsmouth and soon that, too, was flourishing. Both were destroyed by enemy bombing in World War II, but have since been replaced by fine modern buildings, which are considered to be the most up-to-date Services' clubs in the United Kingdom. Newer Rests have been opened at Portland, Gosport, Faslane and Yeovilton.

During her career as the 'Sailors' Friend', it is said, she was once lecturing to a naval audience about the exploits of the famous Roman general Pompey. When she came to describe his fate at the hands of an assassin, she was interrupted by one of the sailors who, presumably carried away by the story, exclaimed loudly, 'Poor old Pompey!' Ever since then the name has stuck to Portsmouth. Much more likely, however, is the theory of other learned historians who aver that the nickname originated from the inebriated libertyman's slurred pronunciation of Portsmouth Point, a locality near the harbour known as the Wapping of Portsmouth whose taverns were particularly popular with sailors.

'Chats' is said to have been derived from an old word meaning 'louse', the inference being that Chatham-manned ships were lousy. But early dictionaries may be fruitlessly combed in search of proof. Although it is a fact that in the days when warships were manned entirely from one Port Division, Chatham-manned ships were sometimes derogatively referred to by sailors from the other two ports as being 'happy and chatty'. The true answer is probably the most obvious – that 'Chats' is simply short for Chatham.

'Guzz' or 'Guzzle' for Devonport is much easier to explain. For this nickname was conferred by grateful sailors who, after languishing at sea for lengthy periods on poor and insufficient victuals, were able when they put into that port to tuck into the tasty and plentiful food traditionally associated with the West Country. As mentioned earlier, one particular delicacy common to that part of the world, the meat and potato pasty, was for long a popular dish in the Navy, and especially Devonport-manned ships, under the name of *tiddy-oggie*, a variant of *taty-oggie*. Incidentally, Devonport-manned ships were usually nicknamed 'Jago's', the term deriving from the name of an officer of the former Accountant Branch who started the general messing system in Devonport naval barracks when further trials of the system were resumed. Lieutenant Jago was chiefly instrumental for the eventual success of this form of messing.

Of the three former Port Divisions, now no longer referred to as such under the Navy's revised system of centralised drafting, Portsmouth was considered to be the senior, and its dockyard boasts the world's oldest dry dock. In the time of Henry VIII the official Keeper of this wonder of the age received the munificent salary of one shilling (5p) per week. Chatham comes next in antiquity and seniority, although Woolwich and Deptford were near rivals when they for a time were Royal dockyards. Chatham dockyard originated back in 1547 when a storehouse for the king's ships was rented beside the Medway for the modest sum of thirteen shillings and fourpence (66½p), and a grounding, or 'graving' place constructed in 1584. Soon after that more warships were being refitted at Chatham than at Portsmouth. As a visible link with the past, some of the roads in the dockyard are still paved with iron ballast blocks that once were carried in the old 'wooden walls'. Devonport, as we have seen, is the youngest of the three home ports, although its dockyard was founded in 1689.

Why, it may be asked, do the Navy's 'stone frigates', a term applied to all naval shore establishments no matter how far from the sea they may be situated, bear ship names? The reason is chiefly one of naval law. Thus in order to bring every officer and rating serving in the Royal Navy under the Naval Discipline Act and to justify expenditure on his victualling and pay, he was required to be borne on ship's books, the Navy's pay ledgers. In fact, no officer or rating was considered to have any official existence unless so borne. This requirement extended even to troops and civilian passengers carried in ships. The Muster Book of HMS *Bellerophon*, the British warship on board which Napoleon was embarked after Waterloo, has the entry, 'General Napoleon and suite' as having been borne on its ration strength as prisoners. On the surviving page of this book, now preserved in the Public Record Office, the words *'Vive l'Empereur!'* have been added by some unknown sympathiser.

Every shore establishment must therefore bear the name of an actual vessel afloat and appearing in the Navy List. For instance, HMS *Pembroke*, the ship name of the Royal Naval Barracks at Chatham, was for a time a renamed trawler, then an ageing harbour launch moored in the nearby naval dockyard. Until comparatively recently officers appointed to serve in the Ministry of Defence (Navy) were borne on the books of HMS *President*, the former Flower class sloop *Saxifrage*, moored alongside the Thames Embankment.

But it is not only to comply with the requirements of naval law that the Navy's shore establishments have to bear a ship's name: it also enables them to benefit from certain traditional customs concessions, such as duty-free wines, liquor and tobacco. Today, as we have seen, these concessions are not so generous as in the past, but their continuation is thus ensured.

In 1957, however, the Naval Discipline Act was amended, and the old-time requirement of being 'borne on ship's books' was abolished. The amended Act states that, 'Every officer on the active list of officers and every rating of the Royal Navy is subject to this Act at all times ...' Today ships' pay ledgers themselves no longer exist, their place having been taken by a computer. Even so, the shore establishment at Gosport in which the computer itself is housed, bears the ship name HMS *Centurion* and is regarded as a 'warship' in full commission.

Three geographical islands have actually served as 'stone frigates' in the Navy's past history. They are Ascension, Tristan Da Cunha and Diamond Rock.

In 1815 when Napoleon was incarcerated on St Helena, a naval garrison was sent to Ascension to deny that island to any would-be rescuers of the fallen dictator. The tip of an extinct volcano, Ascension Island rises out of the South Atlantic almost exactly half-way between Africa and the eastern bulge of South America. With a naval captain as superintendent, the island, while not shown in the Navy List as an independently commissioned warship, was nevertheless a full-blown tender to HMS *Flora*, then the base ship for the Cape of Good Hope station at Simonstown. The island's 'complement' of 109 officers, ratings and Royal Marines included a cowman and shepherd, since it was required to be largely self-supporting, a carter and stableman, and two ratings whose task it was to oversee the periodical turtle boat. For large numbers of turtles visit Ascension regularly to lay their eggs, and up until comparatively recent times turtles from Ascension were despatched to London in British warships, which specially called in for them, to be made into turtle soup for the Lords of the Admiralty.

Tristan Da Cunha, another volcanic peak thrusting out of the South Atlantic, lies some 1800 miles west of Capetown. In case this island, too, might become a base of operations for attempts to rescue Napoleon, a military garrison of 40 officers and men was sent there in 1816 together with their families, totalling 17 women and children. Within a year, however, the garrison was withdrawn, but an artillery corporal and his wife elected to remain. The couple were later joined by two ex-Navy men and a number of shipwrecked sailors. The newcomers found romance through the good offices of the captain of a visiting ship who brought them wives from St Helena, and in due course a thriving little community developed.

Then in 1942 the Navy took over Tristan, whose population knew little of the world war then raging. A surgeon lieutenant-commander RNVR, in peacetime a general practitioner from the Midlands, arrived first with his wife and family, later to become commanding officer of the new 'stone frigate'. First known as 'Job Nine', Tristan was officially commissioned as HMS *Atlantic Isle* on 15th January 1944, by which time a mixed 'crew' of naval communications and other ratings, army engineers and a meteorological staff had arrived and settled in to their newly built quarters, which included a small hospital and twelve houses for married personnel. HMS *Atlantic Isle* was formally paid off in May 1946 when the White Ensign was finally hauled down.

Diamond Rock, situated close to the French island of Martinique

The commissioning ceremony in H.M.S. 'Atlantic Isle', 15 January 1944.

in the West Indies, entered the Royal Navy as a 'sloop of war' in 1804 to embark on a far more exciting 'commission'. Britain was then at war with France, and Commodore Samuel Hood in the 74-gun *Centaur* was blockading the port of Fort Royal in Martinique, one of the last French possessions in the West Indies. Hood noticed that French ships were able to pass freely in and out of Fort Royal through the channel between Diamond Rock and the coast of Martinique.

Diamond Rock rises abruptly from the Caribbean to a height of some 570 feet. It is barren and uninhabited, and the French thought it unscalable. Furthermore, they considered that even if men could be put ashore, the surf, local currents and the steepness of the Rock would make the landing of supplies difficult. It was also within range of shore batteries on Martinique. But Hood perceived that occupation of the island would render blockade by sea unnecessary, and would also close the port of Fort Royal to all large vessels. Accordingly with consummate skill and seamanship he landed 125 sailors and marines on the Rock, together with heavy guns, ammunition, food and water. From January 1804 to June 1805 HMS *Diamond Rock*, a 'stone frigate' with teeth, harassed the

French in Martinique. Not only did its garrison deter ships from trying to enter Fort Royal, they periodically swooped on the harbour to cut out vessels and destroy shore installations.

Finally when Admiral Villeneuve arrived at Martinique from Toulon with his squadron in May of that year in an elaborate feint designed to draw Nelson away from Napoleon's planned invasion of this country, he was persuaded to take time off to neutralise HMS *Diamond Rock*. The operation involved the French admiral in three days and two nights of heavy fighting before the British garrison was forced to retire to the top of their eyrie. Even so, it was only because they had run out of water and small arms ammunition that they were compelled to surrender. As well as valuable time, Villeneuve lost 500 men and several gunboats, and a number of his larger vessels were severely damaged by the 'stone frigate's' gunfire.

Today Diamond Rock is once more inhabited only by the birds, snakes and other small creatures which manage to survive on the island. In 1965 a party of sailors and marines from the frigate HMS *Rothesay*, who climbed to the summit of the island, found no trace of the original 'Governor's House', living quarters for the men, or the hospital and signal station erected by the crew of HMS *Diamond Rock* 174 years ago. But whenever any British warship passes close enough to the island, her boatswain's pipe shrills in salute, albeit the only response may be the plaintive cry of a seabird; probably, say the superstitious, the spirit of one of those dead and gone Nelsonic sailors.

As a matter of interest, Dead Man's Chest which figures largely in the well known rhyme about old-time pirates who sailed the Spanish Main, is an actual island in the Caribbean. In the days when the Royal Navy maintained a small force of warships in the West Indies, one frigate, finding herself in the vicinity of Dead Man's Chest, solemnly sent ashore a party of fifteen men to land on the island. They took with them the traditional bottle of rum!

Probably the oddest 'stone frigate' in commission today is the Admiralty Reactor Test Establishment at Dounreay, thirty miles from John O'Groats. In recognition of the part that establishment plays in the training of future submarine crews, the Admiralty Board in 1970 granted it the functional title of 'Royal Naval Nuclear Propulsion Test and Training Establishment' and the ship name HMS *Vulcan*. One thousand feet up in the foothills of the eastern Pennines another curious 'stone frigate' is HMS *Forest Moor*, which comprises two naval wireless stations. Occupied by the Army during the Second World War, the establishment covers 850 acres of rough moorland, some twelve miles from Harrogate, and its 'ship's company' consists of three officers and 62 ratings, all volunteers.

Although a 'stone frigate' seems far removed in every way from an actual man-of-war, the derivation of the term is not hard to seek. Despite being fashioned of brick and stone, they are run on almost exactly the same lines as a warship. In the grounds of the larger establishments the colourful figureheads which once adorned the bows of name ships of the past are carefully preserved and mounted in prominent positions to remind newer generations of sailors of their illustrious heritage. Traditional shipboard terms are used within the confines of such establishments as far as possible and commensurate with commonsense. Thus each boasts a 'quarterdeck', albeit this may be only a specially defined patch of manicured lawn or brushed gravel close to the flagstaff from which the White Ensign is flown daily, the latter being hoisted in the mornings and lowered at sunset each day with due shipboard ceremonial.

The 'ship's company' ratings, or 'barrack stanchions', as distinct from the floating population of new entries, trainees and the crews of ships refitting, are divided into port and starboard watches; officers and men speak of 'going ashore' when they walk out of the gates on leave; officers' names listed in the wardroom ante-room are so exhibited as to indicate at a glance whether their owners are 'ashore' or 'on board'; the floors of messes, offices and accommodation blocks are always referred to as 'the deck'; bells are struck to denote the passage of time as in a fully commissioned ship afloat; and the duty officer is the 'Officer of the Watch' or 'Officer of the Day'.

Hammock hooks and slinging rails are, however, no longer a feature of the modern high-rise accommodation blocks which since the war have replaced the ageing and bomb-damaged buildings in the naval barracks and technical training establishments. Hammocks, first used in the Navy in 1597, had before the war been replaced by beds ashore, and in the early 1950s they finally disappeared from seagoing ships in favour of tubular steel and

A battleship of the Victorian Navy. Note the hammocks in the upper deck nettings.

canvas bunks for all ratings.

With the disappearance of the hammock, or 'Mɪcᴋ, the sailor's friend' as it was affectionately termed, also went a hoary old naval jape. Thus generations of new entries, having wrestled more or less successfully with the intricacies of slinging a nautical bed, have stood forlornly by it wondering how on earth to board the thing. Although invariably when their dilemma was observed by some seasoned salt, they have been kindly directed to the boatswain's store to draw their 'hammock ladder' – an item as non-existent as the fabulous 'golden rivet' or 'key of the starboard watch'.

The British sailor's hammock also added an unpleasantly bodeful phrase to the English language. For in sailing warships nettings ran round the outboard side of the bulwarks in which the men's hammocks were stowed daily to act as shot-stoppers in action and to provide protection against splinters. If the ship should be sunk such hammocks as were blown overboard made convenient floating rafts for survivors. In order to perform these extramural functions effectively, however, they had to be lashed up tightly, and one of the duties of the old-time master's mates was to pass each man's hammock through a narrow-gauge hoop every morning. Woe betide those whose hammocks failed to negotiate this 'needle's eye'. It is from this one-time nautical practice that the familiar expression to be 'put through' or 'go through the hoop' has been derived.

CHAPTER VI

Navy Rigs

When a sailor talks about 'slops' he is not referring to a semi-liquid diet for infants and invalids. He means items of uniform dress purchased from the purser (pronounced 'pusser') – today the ship's supply officer – or the clothing store. Incidentally, a sailor who habitually obtained all his uniform requirements from this source would be said by his mates to be 'pusser-built', a derogatory term which is also applied to an individual who sticks rigidly to the regulations at all times.

The word 'slop' is defined *inter alia* in most modern dictionaries as 'ready-made clothing, clothes and bedding issued to sailors in the navy', and comes from the ancient word *sloppe* or *slyppe*, meaning a loose garment, wide baggy trousers or breeches. In Chaucer's day *sloppe* meant simply a kind of breeches, and in old Norse was spelt *sloppr*. A manuscript account of the wardrobe of Queen Elizabeth I contains an order to a John Fortescue for the delivery of Naples fustian for 'Sloppe for Jack Green, our Foole'. In the Navy, as we shall see, the word in its present guise and definition first came into official use at the beginning of the seventeenth century.

In the early days of Britain's sea service there was no standard dress for sailors; they wore much the same clothes as landsmen, fashion being dictated by the nature and peculiarities of shipboard life. King Alfred has been called the 'Father' of the Royal Navy, chiefly because he was the earliest English monarch to realise that the first and only real defence of an island lies in sea power. Accordingly he built his own fleet of galleys and trained the crews to man them in order to repel the marauding Norsemen at sea before they could set foot ashore.

The next English king to recognise the importance of having a navy to tackle our seaborne enemies on their own element was Edward the Confessor. But instead of building his own ships, he

'Shipmen' of the Cinque Ports navy.

chartered those belonging to the Barons of the Cinque Ports in return for the grant of certain privileges, and these can be considered as constituting the country's first permanent naval force. Their crews, or 'shipmen', wore a uniform consisting of a tunic of coarse woollen cloth dyed blue, drawers, stockings and shoes.

The blue colour of their dress was a form of camouflage, which had its origins as far back as the Roman occupation of Britain, when small fast sailing craft known as *pictae* patrolled off our coasts to bring intelligence of the approach of hostile vessels. The dark blue colour of their sails and the clothes worn by the crews lessened the chances of being seen by day or night. In the sixteenth century we learn from Hakluyt's *Voyages* that British mariners setting forth in search of the North-East and North-West Passages to the East wore 'a livery of Watchet', sky-coloured cloth so-called from the town of that name in Somerset where the material was made. But blue did not become the standard colour for the Navy man's dress for many years.

Britain's sea service continued to be very much a private force run by the Sovereign until the time of the Stuarts. During the reign of Henry VIII the country's naval affairs made great strides. Inheriting many fine ships accumulated by his father, Henry followed a definite naval policy, steadily adding to his fleet until he possessed the largest navy in the world. He not only built ships, he bought others. He introduced the 'great gun' which revolutionised fighting afloat; appointed a Navy Board to look after the construction, repair and victualling of his fleet; established the first 'standing officers'; issued Fighting Instructions for his commanders; and laid down rates of pay for officers and men. But there was no standard dress for them.

The reason was that in those days, and for a long time to come, the bulk of the ships which comprised 'His Majestie's Navie Royall' were not kept in permanent commission. There was thus no need for full-time crews, other than the standing officers whose job was largely ship maintenance when their vessels had been paid off. Prior to the reign of Charles II, flag officers, captains and lieutenants were discharged to the shore as soon as their ships were paid off. As we have seen, crews were recruited as and when required. Thus the man-o'-warsmen of that period continued to

Sailors of Henry VIII's day.

wear pretty much what they liked. Henry VIII provided some sort of uniform in the shape of coats and jackets for his officers and men.

Then in 1623, towards the end of the reign of James I, the 'slop' system was introduced 'to avoyde nastie beastlyness by diseases and unwholesome ill smells in every ship' – a remark which gives a broad hint of the insanitary conditions prevailing at sea, largely due to the king's own neglect of his fleet. Certain articles of clothing made to specifications laid down by the Navy Commissioners were now to be sold on shipboard under the supervision of the purser. These officially approved garments were canvas jackets, waistcoats, cotton drawers, cotton shirts, thrum caps (cloth threaded with hairy worsted for warmth), and neat's (calf) leather shoes. But because of their high cost the men usually had to be ordered by the captain to draw them from the purser's slop chest for sums to be charged against their pay.

The purser bought his slops from a contractor, who was known as the 'slopseller', and was bound by the terms of his contract to allow the purser a percentage on all sales. 'By overcharging the living and the dead the purser added to his commission, and also to the overplus of stock which would become his when the ship paid off. It was hardly in the interest of the captain to interfere as he also made a good thing out of these practices'.*

During the reign of Charles II the range and variety of slops were extended. In 1663 instructions issued by the Lord High Admiral, then the king's brother the Duke of York, detailed the 'cloaths to be worn by seamen'. They comprised Monmouth (thrum) caps, red caps; yarn stockings, Irish stockings, blue shirts, white shirts, cotton waistcoats, blue neckcloths, canvas suits, and shoes, 'which alone are permitted to be sold'. Collars of cambric or linen falling on to the shoulder came in at about this time.

War with France in 1689 called for many more ships to be added to the fleet, and there was more uniformity in dress. At the Battles of Beachy Head in 1690 and La Hogue in 1692 most British seamen wore kersey jackets, blue waistcoats, white petticoat breeches with red stripes, red caps and white neckcloths.

At the beginning of the eighteenth century the official slop organisation had expanded and there was a wide range of clothes of good material at fair prices. To give some idea of the current

* *A Few Naval Terms, Expressions, Traditions & Superstitions*, Beckett.

They fought under Admiral Blake. Sailors of the Cromwellian Navy.

nautical fashions, the items mentioned in an Admiralty contract of 1706 included 'shrunk kersey jackets lined with red cotton, with 15 brass buttons and two linen pockets, the buttonholes stitched with gold-coloured thread' priced at ten shillings and sixpence (52½p); 'waistcoats of Welsh red, plain unlined with 18 brass buttons, holes stitched with gold-coloured thread' at five shillings and sixpence (27½p); 'red kersey breeches with three leather pockets and 13 white tin buttons' at the same price; also 'red-flowered shag breeches' ('shag' a long-napped rough cloth); striped breeches; blue and white checkered linen shirts at three shillings and sixpence (16p); 'ditto drawers' at two shillings and threepence (11p); leather caps faced with red cotton at one shilling and twopence (6p); grey woollen stockings at one shilling and ninepence (9p); and double-soled shoes.

These styles altered considerably, however, towards the end of the century, and blue began to predominate. The jacket, formerly of grey, was now blue, as were breeches and waistcoats; and, popularised by the French Revolution, long trousers began to be worn. The jacket was short, lined with white and decorated with metal buttons embossed with an anchor, with a black silk handkerchief worn round the neck, white stockings, buckled shoes, and a hat of tarred canvas or straw upon which the ship's name was painted. The hat might also be of leather with a turned-up brim to show a coloured lining. Pigtails became fashionable about 1780.

Since the days when the slop system was first introduced, the Navy man had become something of a natty dresser, and when prize money was forthcoming frequently expressed his exuberant fancies in a spending orgy on clothes as well as other, more fleeting, pleasures. Thus for instance, after the capture of the Spanish treasure ship *Hermione* by the British 28-gun frigate *Active* and 18-gun sloop *Favourite* under the command of Admiral Saunders in 1762, when every rating was awarded the sum of £485 in prize money (Saunders himself received £64,693), it was decreed by their jubilant crews that a gold-laced hat should be an indispensable part of their new rig. One man who appeared in a silver-laced one was nearly lynched by his shipmates, until he explained that all the gold-laced hats had been bought, but he had paid the same money for his silver one! They also bought up all the watches in

Hoisting a signal at Trafalgar.

Portsmouth and fried them over the galley fire to show how little they thought of them.

Seasoned sailors disdained to rig themselves out from the purser's slop chest. There were plenty of civilian tailors on shore in the naval ports eager to cater for their sartorial requirements – forerunners of the famous firm of Gieves (today Gieves & Hawkes), who became outfitters to the Navy in 1785. These merchants kept up with current nautical fashion trends and knew all there was to know about their customers' needs and how to advertise them, as shown by the following sign exhibited above a Portsmouth slopseller's shop in 1790:

MORGAN – MERCER AND SEA DRAPER. No 85 opposite the
Fountain Inn, High Street

Sailors rigged complete from stem to stern, viz. – Chapeau, Napeau, Flying jib and flesh bag; inner pea, outer pea and cold defender; rudder case and service to the same; up haulers, down traders, fore shoes, lacings, gaskets, etc.

> *With canvas bags to hold your cags,*
> *And chests to sit upon,*
> *Clasp knives, your meat*
> *To cut and eat,*
> *When ship does lay along.*

Interpreting these nautical terms: a 'chapeau' was of course a hat; 'napeau' a handkerchief; 'flesh bag' a shirt; 'inner pea' and 'outer pea', different kinds of pea jacket; the 'cold defender' was a woollen comforter; 'rudder case' trousers; 'up haulers' and 'down traders', 'lacings' and 'gaskets' the adaptation of shipboard terms for various tapes and ribbons. A 'cag' was the slang term for a wooden mess drinking utensil. To 'lay along' meant when a ship was in harbour or the hands not required on deck.

By 1800 a fairly general dress for the British Navy man had been evolved. This consisted of a blue jacket (hence the modern term 'bluejacket' for a sailor), sometimes with white tapes sewn along the seams, a loose check shirt, and white trousers, either long or bell-mouthed for rolling above the knee, or short to show a fair amount of coloured stocking, and a red or other coloured waistcoat.

The hat was a low-crowned tarpaulin kept black and glossy with tar and oil, sporting a broad black ribbon with the ship's name on it. A black silk handkerchief was worn around the neck, partly to protect the coat from the greased pigtail and partly for use as a sweat-rag in action. Pigtails continued to be worn on the lower deck up to about 1820 after officers had ceased to sport them. Straw hats were first worn on the West Indies station in 1802, and spread through the Navy as the 'sennet' hat, which was worn up to 1921 when it was replaced by the tropical helmet.

The official *Instructions to Pursers* issued in 1824 contained a lengthy list of clothing of which they were required to maintain a stock on board. Included in the list were blue cloth jackets, knitted worsted waistcoats, blue cloth trousers, white duck trousers and frocks (jumpers), shirts, stockings, hats, and black silk handkerchiefs. Although all these articles were available in the ship's stores, there was little or no attempt by captains to encourage uniformity; any decent clothes would pass muster. On the other hand, some captains introduced garments of their own design and at their own expense, to be worn by at least part of the ship's company, especially the crews of their own gig or barge. Anson in 1740 had his boats' crews dressed as Thames Watermen, with a scarlet jacket, blue silk vest and silver badges on their arms.

In October 1805 *The Times* commented:

The *Tribune*, frigate, now attached to the squadron under Sir Sydney Smith, is no less remarkable for gallantry than the coxcombry of her crew. Every man wears a smart round Japan hat with green inside the leaf, a broad gold lace band with the name of the ship painted in front in capital letters; black silk neckerchief, with a white flannel waistcoat bound with blue; and over it a blue jacket with three rows of gold buttons very close together, and blue trousers.

In 1840 the men of the 50-gun frigate *Vernon* were ordered by their captain to wear red serge frocks and red woollen comforters. When the supply of red garments began to run short, they were retained for one watch while the other was ordered to be dressed in blue frocks and comforters. In 1845 Captain Washington of the steam survey vessel *Blazer* (he later became Hydrographer of the Navy)

Eighteenth-century seamen. One sports a pigtail and the other is wearing a 'Monmouth cap'.

dressed his ship's company in blue and white striped guernseys. Accordingly the crew became known as the 'Blazers', from which is derived the term used for the modern garment of today.

Guernseys or guernsey jackets, had come in during the Napoleonic wars, and Nelson was prepared to approve of them as an article of naval slops. In a letter to the Navy Commissioners in 1804 he wrote:

> I must beg leave to observe that the quality of the said Guernsey jackets is most excellent, but that they are considerably too narrow and short to be tucked into the Men's trowsers. It is therefore my opinion that they ought to be three inches wider and six longer. Indeed, if they were ten inches or a foot, it would be so much better, as they shrink very considerably in washing; and when the Seamen are on the yards, reefing or furling sails, the jacket rubs out of their trowsers, and exposes them to great danger of taking cold in their loins; so that with this alteration, which is particularly necessary, they certainly would be the best and most valuable slops that ever were introduced into the Service.

Captain Wilmott of the brig *Harlequin* was probably anything but popular when he dressed his boat's crew as harlequins; those of the *Tulip* were compelled to wear green coats with a flower in the cap; and in 1851 the men of HMS *Caledonia* were decked out with Scots bonnets embellished with a tartan ribbon. The craze for eccentricity reached its peak when Captain 'Nobby' Ewart, discovering one morning the stroke oar of his boat sporting a ripe black eye, ordered the rest of the crew to paint one eye black! But much of this nautical sartorial nonsense was soon to come to an end.

Three years after the introduction of pensionable continuous service for the men of the lower deck in 1853, the Admiralty set up a select committee to examine the desirability of introducing a uniform dress for seamen. Its chairman was a character in his own right. He was Rear-Admiral (later Admiral) the Hon. Henry J. Rous who in 1855 had been appointed Public Handicapper to the Jockey Club. He held this post for the next thirty years, during which he came to be regarded as the 'dictator of the Turf', his one aim being to keep racing clean and awe offenders. 'The admiral's bold and manly form, erect and stately, dressed in a pea jacket, wearing long black boots or leggings, with dog whip in hand, ready to mount his old bay horse for the course no matter what the weather might be, was an imposing sight at Newmarket'. As a former Lord of the Admiralty, Rous duly whipped his committee into action, their report came out at the end of the year, was adopted and put into effect early in 1857. But even then Their Lordships merely 'desired' that regulated articles of dress should be worn.

According to the Admiralty Circular issued on 30th January of that year, these were to consist of a double-breasted blue cloth jacket, blue cloth trousers fitting tight at the waistband, with two pockets and a broad flap; a duck or white drill frock with collar and wristbands of blue jean, 'each having a border of three rows of white tape'; duck trousers similar to the blue; a blue serge frock; a pea jacket of blue Flushing; black silk handkerchief; and a hat, black or white according to the climate, 'four inches high in the crown, three inches wide in the rim, and seven inches across the crown, made of sennet covered with brown Holland, painted black with a hat ribbon bearing the ship's name'. A second cap was also provided, to be worn at night and at sea when ordered. Made of partially stiffened blue cloth, it was similar in shape to that worn by naval officers without the peak. The final item of the new kit was a dark blue woollen comforter.

The cost of these garments, the first issue to new entries being free, was seventeen shillings and eightpence ($88\frac{1}{2}$p) for the blue cloth jacket; eleven shillings and sevenpence (58p) for the blue cloth trousers; five shillings and fourpence ($26\frac{1}{2}$p) the blue serge frock; two shillings and ninepence (14p) the duck frock; and two shillings and sevenpence (13p) the duck trousers. The black silk cost two shillings and tenpence (14p), and shoes six shillings and sevenpence (33p). Two years later a kit upkeep allowance was introduced.

There is no evidence in the committee's report to uphold the widely held belief, still current even today, that the black silk was introduced to commemorate the death of Nelson, or that the tapes on collar (and cuffs) represented his three great naval victories. As we have seen, neckerchiefs of black or other coloured material had

Bluejacket of 1849 wearing a collar similar to that in use today.
First-Class Petty Officer, circa 1896, wearing serge frock with gold badges
and a sennet hat.

for years been used by sailors as a sweat-rag when working at the guns and as an article of dress.

As to the three rows of tape on the collar, the Rous Committee originally suggested two, but before taking action the Admiralty consulted the Commanders-in-Chief at Portsmouth and Devonport, who in turn obtained the views of the crews of various ships in those ports. Four of the nine ships' companies consulted at Portsmouth opted for two rows of tape, and five for three. At Devonport opinion was unanimously in favour of three: accordingly three it was. Tapes had in fact begun to be worn in the 1830s, and an official Admiralty Circular of 1845 authorised the issue of blue jean and Dutch tape to the crews of HM ships for the purpose of having blue collars, cuffs and facings made to their duck frocks when required. It is not known when the broad collar came into use, but is believed to be some time in the 1830s, although it did not assume its familiar square shape we know today until 1860.

As time went on various changes were made in the uniform of the British sailor, the most distinctive being the introduction in 1879 of a special dress with a peaked cap for the rating of chief petty officer which had been created in 1853. Prior to this they had worn blue-jacket's rig with a special arm badge. The new garb was the forerunner of that worn today by chief and petty officers.

In 1891 a similar type of dress, with black horn buttons on the jacket instead of gilt, and a red embroidered cap badge, was introduced for junior non-seaman categories, men who in Nelson's day and earlier had been termed 'idlers' since they were excused night watches. Later they became officially known as 'Daymen'. The three types of dress were now codified as 'Class I' – chief and petty officers of all branches except petty officers, second class; 'Class II' – men dressed as seamen; and 'Class III' – men not dressed as seamen.

In 1956 another change came about when by popular desire most of the latter reverted to Class II uniform, despite the fact that the bluejacket was said to 'dress like a horse', i.e., 'Everything goes over me head except me boots!'

Sailors traditionally refer to their uniforms as 'rigs', and this is another link with the old days of sail; for a ship was then fitted with a 'suit' of sails and the manner in which these were worn, depending on the class of ship, constituted the 'rig' of the vessel.

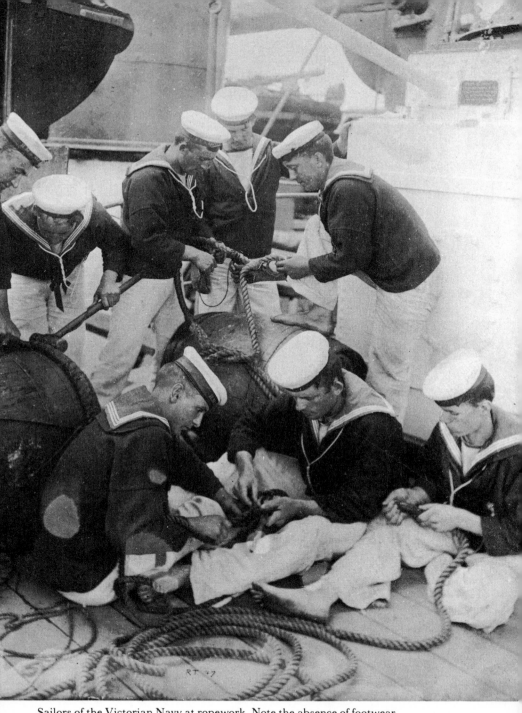

Sailors of the Victorian Navy at ropework. Note the absence of footwear.

A petty officer of 1830 holding a capstan bar.

Thus ratings in Class I dress wear 'fore and aft rig', and the bluejacket, or Class II man, 'square rig'. Since all naval uniforms for both officers and ratings are numbered and described in full detail in the official Uniform Regulations, the sailor's best shoregoing rig is always referred to as his 'Number Ones'.*

We now come to the origin of the word 'tiddly' used to describe the snappy naval dresser, and as a nautical adjective for anything smart and fashionable, e.g., a 'tiddly' ship; 'tiddly' suit; 'tiddly' haircut, and so on. The explanation is simple. It does not mean, as defined in dictionaries of slang, a person who is the worse for wear alcoholically speaking. In the naval sense it was first dreamed up in the 1920s by some anonymous shipboard wag who deliberately mispronounced the word 'tidily' as 'tid-i-ly' in three syllables, 'tid' being pronounced the same as 'bid'.

The uniform regulations of 1857 established the cap ribbon as an official article of dress for the first time. History is reticent about the birth of this small but important item of naval uniform. It is probable that individual captains introduced some form of distinguishing badge or emblem to be displayed on the headgear of their crews so that they could easily be picked out from a crowd of sailors ashore in a fleet anchorage, or on active service in one of the many naval brigades which over the centuries served on shore in support of the Army.

When the shape of the hat currently in vogue allowed, the name of a man's ship was either painted directly on it or on a ribbon bound round it. On the new type of standard cap ribbon now introduced, which was a black silk strip, the ship's name was still painted, but in 1868 gilt wire lettering was introduced, and continued right up to the outbreak of the Second World War.

Successive uniform regulations required the ribbon to be 45 inches long and one and three sixteenths of an inch broad, with the name of the ship embroidered in gilt wire half an inch deep. The centre of the lettering was ordered to be worn over the nose and the bow over the left ear, but when they could get away with it, sartorial deviationists sported the most elaborate bow they or their girl friend could contrive, worn over the left eye. The ends of the ribbon forming the bow were cut into neat swallowtails, and a coin

* The idea of numbering the uniform dresses was to make it easy to signal the 'rig of the day'.

A seaman boy of the 1860s showing the type of cap ribbon worn.

or small button often inserted into the centre to preserve its shape and symmetry. Although frowned on by authority, this became one of the hallmarks of a 'tiddly' sailor, or 'taut hand'.

During hostilities, however, the disposition of units of the Fleet take on a vital secrecy, and during both world wars in order to conceal the movements of individual warships from the prying eyes of enemy agents, nominal cap ribbons were replaced by others bearing the anonymous letters 'H.M.S.'. Production difficulties and shortage of material during the Second World War brought about the disappearance of gilt wire lettering 'for the duration', a deprivation which lingered on for some years afterwards.

At one time it was the charming custom that when a sailor got married he presented a shining new cap ribbon to each bridesmaid, which the young ladies promptly made into a special garter. The late Admiral Lord Mountevans – 'Evans of the *Broke*' – followed this custom by giving each of the six bridesmaids at his wedding in 1917 one of the original sailor's cap ribbons issued to the crew of the *Terra Nova*, the ship in which he accompanied Captain Scott on the latter's last expedition to the South Pole. At an auction sale many years afterwards one of these ribbons fetched a handsome sum of money.

As many tailors were press-ganged into the Navy in the days when this form of forcible recruitment was the principal means of manning the Fleet, they frequently followed their trade on board by repairing and making articles of clothing for their shipmates. When the sewing machine was invented, shipboard 'jewing firms', as they were known, who usually took their own machine, or 'donkey', with them from ship to ship, continued to flourish. Following the establishment of a standard uniform for sailors in 1857, it became possible for individuals to buy a length – usually six yards – of blue serge in lieu of readymade clothing from the ship's store in order to have their best Number One suits made to measure on board by the ship's jewing firm. It was then that the practice began of making flowing bell-bottomed trousers, because it was easier to use the full width of the material. Since a bolt of serge measured 54 inches across, this, allowing for turn-ins, just made two trouser legs. The shipboard jewing firm and his 'donkey' have long since vanished from the mess decks of British warships, but they could still be found in the Fleet as late as the 1920s.

Physical training exercises on the quarterdeck of a Victorian battleship. Note the duck suits worn by the men.

Even royalty on one occasion patronised a shipboard jewing firm. When in 1848 Queen Victoria and her Consort embarked in the royal yacht for a cruise to a number of places in Devon, Cornwall and the Channel Islands, they took their seven-year old son Prince Albert Edward along. The Queen wrote in her journal: 'Bertie put on his sailor's dress which was beautifully made for him on board by the men who make for our sailors.' While the young prince was not to follow the sea as a profession, he did however, thus popularise the sailor suit for small boys of all classes.

It is interesting to compare the 'tiddly' sailor of earlier times with his counterpart of later days. Thus the naval hero of a novel called *Ben Brace* by Captain Frederick Chamier in 1836 is described as being: 'In smart attire with his tail (pigtail) down to his sternpost, ducks tight round the waist with enough canvas in the legs of them to dress an Irish family, and a pair of sailor's shoes with about a yard of ribbon in each'.

The sailor of the 1920s and 1930s easily rivalled Chamier's hero.

Leading Patrolman (now called Leading Regulators) in 1956 rig.

The V-neck of the blue serge jumper, made to measure and fitting tightly at waist and cuffs, was cut as wide and low as possible. The pale blue jean collar, which had been washed over and over again in order to produce the much-desired faded look indicative of a 'staid hand', bore knife-edged creases obtained by pressing it between the covers of its owner's *Seamanship Manual*, since there were then no electric irons on shipboard. The black silk handkerchief, illegally cut in half to make it less bulky, was folded thinly, pressed and kept in place by the long swallow-tailed tapes of the jumper.

The uniform flannel vest – forerunner of the modern T-shirt – was replaced for shoregoing purposes by a flannel or cotton 'dickey', secured with tapes around the chest; no 'taut hand' of those days would have been found dead wearing a 'pusser's flannel' on leave. The full-bottomed trousers were 'laddered' – a special method of creasing attained by turning the trouser legs inside out, damping, and folding each individually concertina fashion. Since as has been said, ironing was impossible, the creases were retained in position and enhanced by securing the folded trousers within two stiff cardboard covers tied with a spare lanyard until required for wear. Although a white lanyard was officially *de rigueur*, and with a jack-knife on the end of it, this, too, was promptly discarded when out of sight of authority.

The finishing touch was provided by the cap. The customary unsightly stiffening grommet was removed, and the edge of the crown then stitched all round to produce the special shape and style which distinguished the seasoned tar from the new entry, or 'nozzer'.

Although undeniably smart in appearance, all such sartorial niceties and embellishments were, unhappily, contrary to regulations. Nevertheless persistence eventually paid off, for in the 1950s various official innovations were made to smarten up the uniform of the British bluejacket, which in essence has been copied by every other navy. Form-fitting, coat-style, zip-fronted jumpers made of diagonal serge cloth were introduced, along with zip-fastened trousers fitted with side and hip pockets in place of the old-time flap front. Another innovation was a plastic-topped white cap needing no stiffening grommet for both officers and men, to be worn all the year round at home and abroad. Previously blue caps had been worn in the winter months in home waters.

It is from the gradual evolution of the sailor's uniform that the naval expression 'make and mend', used today to denote a half holiday from work, has been derived. The stocks of slop clothing carried on board the old-time sailing warships were necessarily limited; moreover the sailor could draw his pay only at the end of a ship's commission, which might drag on for years. Reluctant to squander any part of his hard-earned money on 'pusser's slops', he preferred to make his wardrobe last out for as long as possible. In order to give their men an opportunity to repair their garments or fashion new ones, captains of ships began to set aside one afternoon a week – usually on Thursdays – for this purpose. On such days, known as 'rope yarn Sundays', the boatswain's mates would pipe the hands to 'make and mend clothes'. This expression has remained in current use in the British Navy, notwithstanding that the modern sailor no longer has to rely on his own skill with a needle or that of his shipmates for the upkeep of his uniform.

CHAPTER VII

'To distinguish sea officers'

The supremacy of British sea power was fairly firmly established by the middle of the eighteenth century and, for officers at least, the Navy had become a full time profession. Yet Britain was the only European nation whose naval officers lacked a uniform. The nearest any of her sea officers had come to this was when James I by Warrant of 6th April 1609 granted to six of his principal Masters of the Navy 'Liverie coats of fine red cloth'. This Warrant was drawn verbatim from one signed by Queen Elizabeth but which had not been acted on by reason of her death. But King James' red livery was soon discontinued.

British admirals and captains therefore wore what they pleased, sporting a variety of flamboyant rigs, with coats of military cut in crimson, green or blue; red faced with blue or blue faced with red being the most popular. This costume was usually topped off with a three-cornered hat trimmed with gold lace and adorned with a cockade, a form of headgear said to have been introduced by George I. Since there was no uniform pattern of sword, they wore whatever weapons they chose.

Admiral Thomas Mathews, Commander-in-Chief, Mediterranean Fleet until he was sacked for allegedly mishandling an engagement with a French and Spanish squadron off Toulon in 1744, wore a blue coat with gold lace and a red waistcoat. Round about the same period Captain Windham, commanding HMS *Kent*, and his officers favoured green coats faced with red with a red waistcoat and breeches. Commodore Charles Brown, second in command at Vernon's capture of Porto Bello, lived up to his name by affecting a complete outfit of russet brown; while a Captain Whipple, who was probably a keen hunting enthusiast when ashore, wore a pink coat.

The need for a uniform had, however, been felt for some time, and in 1745 a number of officers belonging to the Navy Club, which used to meet in Will's Coffee House in Scotland Yard, put their heads together and decided to petition the king, then George II, for a standard dress for naval officers. The leading lights in this move were Captains Augustus Keppel and Philip Saumarez and Admiral the Hon. John Forbes.

There are several versions as to what happened next. One story has it that when these three representatives of the Navy Club waited upon the First Lord of the Admiralty with their suggestion, the latter, then the fourth Duke of Bedford, asked them to appear at the Admiralty in uniforms of their own design which could then be shown to the king for him to make a choice. While there is no trace of this modelling session ever having been held, Captain Saumarez and his companions, however, designed an outfit of blue and white which they induced the Duchess of Bedford to wear when she next went riding in the park. She did and was duly seen by the king, who had an eye for a pretty woman, and he approved of the colours for the Navy.

Another story is that when Admiral Forbes was called in by George II to discuss a design for a naval uniform, he suggested a mixture of red on blue or blue on red as being the national colours. But the First Lord told him that the king had already chosen blue and white, having seen the Duchess riding in the park wearing a dark blue and white habit, and he considered this most suitable for the uniform of the Royal Navy.

In his book *A Silver-Plated Spoon** the present Duke of Bedford, referring to the life of the fourth duke when First Lord of the Admiralty, states that:

> One of the most fascinating relics is a bill for a blue and white habit for one of his daughters, Lady Caroline Russell. The duchess must have had a similar outfit, as an anecdote is recounted of when Admiral the Hon. John Forbes had been called in by George II to discuss a design for a naval uniform, he suggested a mixture of red and blue as being the national colours. The duke told him of the king's decision: 'The King is determined otherwise, for having seen my Duchess riding in the park a few days ago in a habit of dark blue faced with white, the

* Cassell & Co.

dress took the fancy of his Majesty, who has appointed it for the uniform of the Royal Navy'.

Whatever the truth of these stories, the fact is that blue and white was the choice of George II for the colour of the Navy's present day uniform.

Curiously enough, the actual order for the introduction of a uniform, 'the better to distinguish the rank of sea officers', for admirals, captains, commanders, lieutenants and midshipmen, dated 13th April 1748, was never gazetted or issued as an Order-in-Council. Patterns of clothing for flag officers could be seen at the Admiralty, for captains downwards at the Navy Office and at Plymouth, but none were sent abroad. This led Admiral Boscawen, then commanding-in-chief in the East Indies, to write plaintively in February 1749 that he could not comply with the order as he was entirely at a loss regarding the pattern.

At first the new uniform conformed largely to costumes of the period worn on shore, but of the distinctive colours which had taken the fancy of the king, embellished with special buttons and embroidery. For admirals it consisted of an embroidered blue coat down to the knees with white facings, worn unbuttoned; blue breeches, white stockings, and a fancy embroidered waistcoat. There was much gold lace down the front and on the buttonholes. Captains had no lace on the buttonholes and a different type of cuff; lieutenants wore blue slashed cuffs. Midshipmen wore a blue tail coat with white cuffs and collar; the latter could be turned up and fastened by a single button. It was not until 1787 that the round jacket was introduced for midshipmen, with a white patch on the collar known as a 'turnback' or 'weekly account'. At that time the young gentlemen carried a sword and wore a tricorn hat.

But the new uniforms, which were expensive, did not take immediately, the reason being the vague wording and incompleteness of the dress regulations, which rendered their interpretation largely a matter of guesswork. For the next twenty to thirty years it was usual only for admirals, captains and commanders to have their own uniform. In individual ships the lieutenants clubbed together to purchase one coat which they wore in turn, as also did the midshipmen.

Not all captains insisted on the absolute letter of the regulations concerning dress being observed by their officers. But one with notions of his own was Prince William, later the 'Sailor King' William IV. When commanding the fifth-rate *Andromeda* on the Halifax station in 1788, the first of his captain's orders ran as follows:

> With the established uniform, the officers and gentlemen belonging to his Majesty's ship I have the honour to command are, whenever ordered, to appear full dressed, and when sent upon all duties, to wear boots, gold-laced hats and black stocks, and their hair queued constantly; at sea they are permitted to appear in brown breeches, long blue or linen trousers, with or without boots; in the summer and in the West Indies with linen waistcoats and breeches, and nankeen are allowed on board. The lieutenants may wear their frock uniforms, and the gentlemen jackets and round hats except mustering. On the Sunday, pursuant to the new regulations, the master, purser, surgeon, his mates and the clerk are likewise to appear in their uniforms, attending to this order; only they may consider plain hats as their uniform.

By then a uniform had been established for warrant officers, who included masters, surgeons, pursers, gunners, boatswains and carpenters. The Prince also had firm ideas on the form the official uniform should take for the midshipmen.

> It was HRH's pleasure that there should be uniformity, but the dress was of his own imagination and quite at variance from that which the Service prescribed. Old and young, tall and short, all were to be alike; the boy of twelve years old was to be rigged out as a man and squeezed into a tight dress as to leave no chance of growing ... Only conceive a midshipman with white breeches so tight as to appear sewn upon the limb, yellow-topped hunting boots pulled close up and strapped with a buckle round the knee. A pigtail of huge dimensions dangling beneath an immense square gold-laced cocked hat ... and a sword about two-thirds of the little body that wore it. Such was the dress conceived and adopted by our naval captain.*

* *Letters of Admiral of the Fleet Sir T.B. Martin*, Navy Records Society.

Whenever they could, however, the midshipmen sidestepped their captain's commands. But woe betide them if their disobedience should come to his notice, as evidenced by this blast directed at the offenders:

Andromeda, Halifax Harbour, September 1st, 1788.
From my having yesterday met in the town of Halifax several of the gentlemen belonging to his Majesty's ship under my command in shoes and stockings who to my certain knowledge went on shore in the established dress of the ship, it is my particular orders and directions that every officer and gentleman belonging to his Majesty's ship under my command do appear when on leave on shore in their uniform as directed in No.1. It is with equal surprise and astonishment that I am under the necessity of giving this order, having already so repeatedly expressed my wish of uniformity and officer-like appearance in the officers and gentlemen. This order being particularly addressed to them, they are to remember that any person who has the honour to serve in his Majesty's naval service cannot distinguish themselves more properly then by a strict adherence to all written orders and verbal wishes of their commanding officer.

Soon after he became king, William brought in another notion of his own; much to the wrath of the Admiralty he changed the white facings on the uniform of naval officers to red, and thus they remained for ten years, when white was again reintroduced.

Over the years many alterations and innovations have been made to naval officers' uniforms. In 1783 the full dress uniform for flag officers was distinguished by embroidery on the cuffs to denote rank. Thus full admirals wore three rows, vice-admirals two, and rear-admirals one row. Ten years later epaulettes were introduced. Admirals wore two, embellished with silver stars to denote rank; post-captains two of plain gold; junior captains one on the right shoulder only, and commanders one on the left shoulder. Prior to this, epaulettes had been worn unofficially. They were then shaped like a tassel and were known as 'swabs' right up to the date of their abolition in 1950, although by this time they had changed in shape.

The reason for the official introduction of epaulettes into the

Royal Navy was that British naval officers travelling abroad in uniform were not accorded the usual honours by foreign sentries, who did not recognise uniformed individuals without epaulettes as officers. These adornments had been worn for some time in the French and Spanish navies and by our own Royal Marine officers. When Nelson met two of his fellow captains in France wearing epaulettes he thought them 'great coxcombs'. In 1783 he wrote that he considered epaulettes were effeminate and was sure he would dislike them very much if they were introduced into the Navy. When they did come in, he discovered that they improved his appearance!

To commemorate the Glorious First of June battle, George III authorised the introduction of stripes of gold lace on the cuffs; admirals to wear three, vice-admirals two, and rear-admirals one. It was not until 1856 that gold distinction lace for all officers was approved, when captains wore three stripes, commanders two, and lieutenants one. When the rank of sub-lieutenant was created he was given one gold stripe, while his seniors were ordered to add another stripe to those already authorised. It was then that the curl was added to the top stripe of officers of the executive branch. In October 1918 this difference in the gold sleeve lace worn by executive and non-executive officers disappeared, with the exception of the coloured distinction cloth then worn by the latter. Today that, too, has vanished except for medical officers.

The three-cornered hat in turn gave way to the cocked hat, once referred to derisively by the lower deck as a 'top hat with sleeves in', and by the officers themselves as a 'scraper'. This was usually worn in two ways: athwartships for admirals, and fore and aft for other officers. In 1825 when the first *Uniform Regulations for the Fleet* were issued, all officers were ordered to wear the cocked hat fore and aft in both full and undress uniform. At sea a round black hat with a black silk or leather cockade was to be worn.

It would be tedious and outside the scope of this book to record all the variations made since 1748 in the uniform of the British naval officer, which continued to differ from station to station until well into the second half of the nineteenth century. Breeches went out in 1825 except for wear at Royal Drawing Rooms; cap badges came in in 1846. In 1856 midshipmen were issued with a dirk in place of the sword formerly worn, and in 1879 the monkey jacket

Admiral of the Fleet Sir Provo Wallis (1791-1892), 'Father' of the Navy, in his full dress uniform.

was substituted for wear on board in place of the blue tunic.

In 1867 naval aides-de-camp to the Queen wore a crimson and gold sash over the left shoulder. Seven years later Queen Victoria's second son, the Duke of Edinburgh, married the daughter of the Tsar Alexander II of Russia. Following his engagement to her, the Duke was given the honorary rank of captain in the Russian navy. When he visited the court of his future father-in-law he noticed that some of the Russian grand dukes appointed as personal aides-de-camp to the Tsar wore a large gold aiguillette bearing the Tsar's own cypher. The duke liked the idea, and suggested to his mother that the sash worn by her aides-de-camp should be replaced by a gold aiguillette worn over the right shoulder. Queen Victoria approved, and the change was made, but the Royal Cypher was added only in 1920. Later on blue and gold aiguillettes were introduced for staff officers to a commander-in-chief, to be worn over the left shoulder.

This particular sartorial adornment is believed to date back to feudal times as a badge of office, when the horses of a feudal chief and his entourage were picketed close to their tents at night. Each morning when camp was struck it was the duty of one of the retainers to gather up the picket ropes and pegs and carry them with him until they were next required. Since the ropes were wound round the man's body with the pegs hanging down, the whereabouts of the chief could quickly be ascertained by locating this particular henchman, who was invariably to be found in close proximity to his master.

Another addition to the British naval officer's uniform which resulted from the Duke of Edinburgh's appointment in the Russian navy was a greatcoat which up to then had not formed part of standard British kit. In 1890, when he had reached the rank of full admiral, the Duke became chairman of a committee on naval officers' uniform. As a result of their deliberations the first full and detailed dress regulations were issued in the following year. These introduced, *inter alia*, an official boat cloak, made the monkey jacket the normal undress rig for a naval officer, and banished the round hat.

The committee also recommended that admirals of the fleet should wear an aiguillette and receive a baton the same as a field marshal. The aiguillette was approved, but not the baton.

Nevertheless when HRH had himself been promoted to the rank of admiral of the fleet he was presented with a baton by his mother on the occasion of her Diamond Jubilee. But first she had to do battle with the Board of Admiralty, when for once it might be said, she came off second best.

In May 1897 her private secretary informed the First Lord of the Admiralty that her Majesty desired to present a baton to her son, and enquired as to the whereabouts of the baton given to her uncle the Duke of Clarence as admiral of the fleet in 1821. In fact four batons had previously been presented to admirals of the fleet, so the Queen had a perfectly good precedent for the request she was about to make. The first had been given by George IV to his brother William – the subject of the Queen's enquiry – the second in the same year by George IV to Admiral the Earl of St Vincent. In 1830 William gave his baton to Admiral of the Fleet William Peere Williams-Freeman, who was then aged ninety-one; and the fourth was also given by William IV to Admiral Lord Gambier 'as a testimonial of his personal regard and of the estimation in which he holds his long, faithful and meritorious service'. Gambier was by then infirm, suffering and nearly blind, and died in the following year.

A field marshal's baton is a wooden staff, 23 inches long, covered with maroon velvet studded with golden lions, with a flat gold boss at either end, ornamented with a circle of laurel leaves and the rose, shamrock and thistle, with, surmounting the top boss, a modelled representation of St George killing the dragon. The naval version differed only in being covered with blue velvet instead of maroon.

The Queen, however, wanted the Admiralty to meet the cost of the baton she wished to give the Duke of Edinburgh. But the Admiralty demurred; they did not approve of batons being carried by admirals of the fleet, and they were backed up in their stand by Garter King of Arms who maintained that it was never the custom for an admiral of the fleet to receive a baton by virtue of his rank as for field marshals.

Victoria therefore ordered one to be made by the Court jewellers and paid for it herself. But when she presented it to her 'dear Affie', as she called her son, she took care to see that the gift was gazetted as having been presented to the Duke *as Admiral of the Fleet*!

The suggestion that a baton should be awarded to admirals of the fleet was revived several times afterwards, but has always been turned down. King George V, who was himself a serving flag officer, was never in favour of the idea. He declared that as he always carried a telescope he would only find a baton an encumbrance, and that anyway he disliked having to carry a baton even when wearing his field marshal's uniform.

By the time of the outbreak of the Second World War naval officers were required to maintain fourteen distinct rigs or 'dresses'. Each was numbered and carefully described in the *Dress Regulations* down to the smallest button, together with a list of the occasions on which to be worn. The Number One full dress was so costly that junior officers were officially excused from providing themselves with it until they attained a certain rate of pay. Comparatively few senior officers even could afford the full range, and sword and cocked hat-borrowing for special occasions was commonplace.

The modern version of the 1748 flag officer's full dress consisted of a double-breasted frock coat of fine blue cloth lined with white kerseymere. The skirts were edged with inch-deep gold lace, the collar piped with gold oak leaves, and the cuffs slashed with white cloth and embroidered with the appropriate gold distinction lace of rank. The trousers were decorated with a wide gold stripe running down each outside leg, dubbed irreverently by the wearers 'lightning conductors', and the epaulettes of pearl and gold lace embroidered with gold oak leaves and acorns, with gold bullions, or 'swabs', pendant from each. The full dress sword belt was of black silk webbing embroidered with gold oak leaves and acorns, and the cocked hat of black beaver with golden tassels and a cockade of bullion.

The Number Two rig was almost as gorgeous as the full dress. It was a super evening dress, consisting of mess jacket with epaulettes, gold-laced trousers, white waistcoat, sword and full dress belt. If the weather was inclement, or a boat trip was entailed, this magnificence would be discreetly covered by the boat cloak. The latter garment was made of blue cloth lined with white silk, with gold or gilt lion-head fastenings and chain at the neck. This dress was prescribed for wear at official balls, dinners, and other public junketings of importance. The quantity and weight of gold lace, bullions, etc., worn varied with the rank of the officer. The footwear for both these rigs was Wellington boots or half-Wellingtons; not, it should be added, the 'Wellies' worn today for gardening or other outdoor work, but hand made of fine leather polished to a mirror finish.

All this naval sartorial magnificence disappeared during the Second World War. In fact it was fated never to return, for in 1950 the Admiralty announced that in view of the continuing post-war austerity there was little likelihood of the reintroduction, even in modified form, of pre-war naval full dress. In future the blue monkey jacket and trousers, or Number Five dress, as it was listed, would constitute the official rig for all occasions, with the addition where appropriate of orders, decorations and medals, and a wing collar and bow tie for more formal affairs. Nine years later, however, a frock coat was again introduced for flag officers, albeit this garment was shorn of much of its former glory, with the ordinary flat cap in place of the pre-war cocked hat; but the old oak leaf-decorated sword belt was restored.

Today, curiously enough, the number of uniform rigs for naval officers has risen to a score in place of the previous fourteen, and includes such innovations and informalities as bush jackets, berets, sandals, and even woolly pullovers with rank epaulettes. As an echo of the past, however, modified ball and mess dresses for evening wear by captains and above have been reintroduced, together with their accompanying special trousers, 'lightning conductors' and all.

CHAPTER VIII

'I name this ship ...'

One very old naval custom which has been revived since the end of the Second World War is the commissioning ceremony for a warship, conducted at the commencement of service of a newly built ship, or one that has been out of commission for a long period owing to refit or reconstruction. It consists of a religious service the origins of which go back in time as far, at least, as the Crusades, and in the standard form given below has once again become part of British naval tradition.

On the appointed day after the ship's commissioning (or 'masthead') pennant has been duly hoisted – to remain flying until she finally pays off – the newly joined captain, officers and ship's company assemble, either on the quarterdeck or on the jetty alongside which the vessel is lying, usually in the presence of a congregation composed chiefly of the wives and families of the new crew. The ship's chaplain, appropriately robed and surpliced, opens the proceedings by addressing the assembly in these words:

'Brothers, seeing that in the course of our duty we are set in the midst of many and great dangers, and that we cannot be faithful to the high trust placed in us without the help of Almighty God, let us unite our prayers in seeking His blessing upon this ship and all who serve in her, that she may sail under God's good providence and protection, and that there may never be lacking men well qualified to offer in her their work and skill for His greater glory, and for the protection of our realm and commonwealth.'

After an appropriate hymn, the chaplain declaims: 'The waves of the sea are mighty and rage horribly'.

Ship's company: 'But yet the Lord who dwelleth on high is mightier'.

The captain then reads the Lesson, which is taken from St Matthew, Chapter VIII, verses 23 to 27, as being the most applicable to the occasion.

This is followed by the 'Bidding', a form of solemn litany between captain and crew, taken from the Gaelic Blessing of 1589.

Captain: 'I call upon you to pray for God's blessing on this ship. Bless our ship.'

Crew: 'May God the Father bless her.'

Captain: 'Bless our ship.'

Crew: 'May Jesus Christ bless her.'

Captain: 'Bless our ship.'

Crew: 'May the Holy Spirit bless her.'

Captain: 'What do ye fear, seeing that God the Father is with you?'

Crew: 'We fear nothing.'

Captain: 'Whom do ye fear, seeing that God the Son is with you?'

Crew: 'We fear nothing.'

Captain: 'What do ye fear, seeing that God the Holy Spirit is with you?'

Crew: 'We fear nothing.'

Then comes the Blessing, which is given either by the chaplain, or by some more important Church dignitary, such as the Chaplain of the Fleet, who may have been invited to the ceremony.

Chaplain: 'Our help is in the name of the Lord.'

Crew: 'Who hath made Heaven and Earth.'

Chaplain: 'The Lord be with you.'

Crew: 'And with Thy spirit.'

Now follow two special prayers.

I. 'O Thou that sittest above the water floods and stillest the raging of the sea, accept, we beseech Thee, the supplication of Thy servants for all who in this ship, now or hereafter, shall commit their lives to the perils of the deep. In all their ways enable them truly and godly to serve Thee, and by their Christian lives to set forward Thy glory throughout the world. Watch over them in their going out and their coming in, that no evil befall them, nor mischief come nigh to hurt their souls. And so through the cares of this troublesome world, and through all the changes and chances of this mortal life, bring them of Thy mercy to the sure haven of Thine everlasting Kingdom.'

II. 'Almighty God, for the sake of his Son, through the comfort of the Holy Ghost, save and sanctify you, and carry you with favouring winds and comfort over the sea and into harbour according to His own will, which thing we desire from Him, saying: Our Father, which art in Heaven, hallowed be Thy name. Thy kingdom come. Thy will be done on earth as it is in heaven. Give us this day our daily bread, And forgive us our trespasses, As we forgive them that trespass against us, And lead us not into temptation, But deliver us from evil; for Thine is the kingdom, The power and the glory, For ever and ever, Amen.'

The ship is then blessed in these words:

'O Lord God Almighty, who blesseth those that put their trust in Thee, let Thy blessing be upon this ship, and upon all who sail and serve in her; May good success and Thy protection and the guardianship of the holy Angels be with them always.'

Three more prayers are now said: the first for the Navy; the second for the upholding of its best traditions; and the third 'For our homes and all who are dear to us', after which comes the final benediction. Pronounced by the Chaplain of the Fleet or other dignitary, it uses the following form of words, which epitomise the spirit in which the Royal Navy has throughout the centuries performed its task of maintaining the *Pax Britannica*:

'Go forth into the world in peace; be of good courage; hold fast to that which is good; render to no man evil for evil; strengthen the fainthearted; support the weak; help the afflicted; honour all men; love and serve the Lord, rejoicing in the power of the Holy Spirit.'

If the ship has been newly built, she will of course have undergone the traditional christening ceremony at her launching. As is well known, this ritual usually involves breaking a bottle of champagne or other suitable liquid over the ship's bows while she is still on the slipway. As the launching lever is pulled, or button pressed, the personage upon whom the honour of launching the vessel has been conferred – usually a lady – utters the words, 'I name this ship – , and may God bless all who sail in her.'

There is an amusing story that on one occasion during World War II of the launch of an American warship by a famous film actress, the lady in question found herself still clutching a sizeable portion of the champagne bottle after the vessel had successfully slid down the ways. Carried away by the occasion, and possible earlier imbibing, she turned to the distinguished naval officer who stood beside her on the launching platform and enthusiastically crowned him with the remains of the bottle, exclaiming as she did so, 'And jolly good luck to you, too, Admiral!'

True or not, the practice of breaking a bottle of wine over the bows of a warship at her launching ceremony was not always followed in Britain. Prior to the reign of William III, it was the custom to drink to the future well-being of a newly built ship from a silver cup, which was afterwards thrown into the sea in order to prevent anyone else drinking from it with ill intent. As this uneconomic procedure added undesirably to the annual naval estimates, it was discontinued and the present practice instituted. Up to the year 1811 British warships were always launched by a Royal personage or a dockyard commissioner. Then the Prince Regent suggested that a lady should have the honour, and this charming custom has remained.

But today the champagne bottle is securely fastened with a lanyard or some other device. For whatever the American film actress may have done, one English lady hurled the bottle at the bows of the ship she was launching with such poor aim that it hit a

Launch of the 131-gun sail and screw battleship *Marlborough* by Queen Victoria at Portsmouth, July 1855.

spectator and put him in hospital. And, of course, this one-time purely naval custom has now been extended to the launch of every newly built vessel, both warship and merchantman – even small yachts.

In Greek and Roman times the launching of a ship was celebrated by pouring out a libation to the gods. The Romans used water to denote purity, and christened their vessels with masculine names; the Greeks chose wine and conferred feminine names on their ships.

Since the modern sailor still retains some of the superstitions of his forebears, any little *contretemps* which may occur to mar a ship's launching ceremony is apt to be noted and recalled should she subsequently encounter misfortune during her seagoing career. For example, when in 1905 the Duchess of Devonshire swung the bottle of champagne against the bows of the new cruiser *Natal*, it continually bounced back at her. At last the exasperated manager of the building yard, who stood next to her, seized the bottle himself and hurled it with such force at the vessel's stem that it smashed to fragments.

Ten years later, by which time the ship's earlier reputation as a lucky vessel had changed to the more sombre one of 'sea hearse', because she was chosen to convey the body of the defunct American Ambassador to Britain back to the United States – carrying a corpse on board being considered extremely unlucky – the cruiser blew up in Cromarty Firth with great loss of life. Not only that: the hoodoo continued to haunt her remains for many years afterwards. No less than four salvage firms which at various times purchased the wreck with the intention of breaking it up for scrap went bankrupt, the fourth losing their salvage vessel with its entire crew in a storm. There have been other cases of ship launchings going awry, but none which seem to have had such peculiarly lingering after-effects.

Before a ship can be christened a name must of course be chosen for her. Today this choice is made by recommendation of the Ships' Names Committee, a body composed of representatives of various departments of the Ministry of Defence (Navy), usually chaired by the Director of Naval Equipment and which includes the Head of the Naval Historical Library.

The practice of conferring names on warships dates back as far at least to the reign of Henry III, when that king's particular 'great ship' was christened the *Queen*, and this is probably the oldest British warship name. Henry V's fleet in which he was conveyed to Harfleur in 1415, from which port he went on to win his great victory at Agincourt, numbered some 1600 vessels, but of these only three 'great ships' had actually been built as fighting vessels. They were named *Jesu, Trinity* and *Holigost*. All the others, carracks, galleys, ballingers and the rest, although called 'King's ships', were in fact hired merchantmen adapted for fighting.

Today the selection of ships' names is regarded as a subject of considerable importance. The major factor is tradition, and it is necessary to go back to the origin of a name to find any justification for its repetition. Here again the superstition of the seaman has to be taken into consideration. Names which have an association with calamity are unpopular, as also, curiously enough, are those of reptiles. Certainly the last three vessels to bear the names *Serpent, Viper* and *Cobra* all came to grief.

The *Serpent*, a third-class 'torpedo cruiser', built in 1887, sailed from Plymouth for Gibraltar in the winter of 1890, and was wrecked two days later on an uncharted rock off Corunna in a gale. There were only three survivors, 173 officers and men being drowned. The *Viper* and *Cobra* were turbine-driven torpedo-boat destroyers, and both were lost in 1901 within a few months of each other. The former went down in August of that year on Burhou Island, near Alderney, in a storm, her crew being saved; and the latter in October during a howling North Sea gale off the Lincolnshire coast, all 67 officers and men being lost.

However around that time torpedo-boat destroyers had acquired an unsavoury reputation for mishaps. When the late King George V, then Lieutenant Prince George, was appointed to command Torpedo Boat *No 79* for the autumn naval manoeuvres of 1889, his mother noted apprehensively on a letter from the flag officer commanding the Prince's squadron, Vice-Admiral Baird, 'The Queen cannot help feeling anxious about her dear son, for torpedo boats are dangerous. Remember how many the French lost five months ago ...' The prince, however, came through the experience without harm, and actually saved one of his consorts from being wrecked.

Yet there had been nine former *Serpents*, 17 *Vipers*, of which four were lost, and six *Snakes*. The name *Rattlesnake*, first used in 1777, was given to an *Algerine* class minesweeper in 1943, and she managed to survive her war service unscathed. There had been eight *Rattlers* since 1783, the last being a fleet minesweeper built during the Second World War. To avoid confusion with the escort carrier *Battler*, however, she was renamed *Loyalty*, but she succumbed to a mine or torpedo in 1944. And of course it was a former *Rattler* which in a tug of war with the paddle steamer *Alecto* in 1860 triumphantly demonstrated to the Admiralty the superiority of the screw propeller over the paddle. Other reptilian names previously used without misfortune were *Adder*, *Crocodile* and *Hamadryad*.

Although many warships have come to grief during their active careers, this does not necessarily bar their names from being used again; but more often the nature and circumstances of the mishaps. *Eagle*, one of the oldest names in the Navy List, but now about to disappear as the last holder, a fleet aircraft carrier, lies in a breaker's yard, is one with a chequered history. There have been 21 holders of the name, the first being the *Eagle of Lubeck*, purchased in 1592. Three successors were vessels taken in prize and expended as fireships. The sixth foundered on passage to St Helena; the seventh was a unit of the ill-fated squadron which, under Admiral Sir Cloudisley Shovell, was returning to England in 1707 when it was caught in a great storm off the Scillies. The *Eagle* with the *Romsey* and the flagship *Association* went down with considerable loss of life. By a miracle the admiral reached the shore alive, only to be knocked on the head by an islander who coveted his emerald ring. The eighth, an advice vessel, was also wrecked in a storm, but the most recent to bear the name more than made up during her career for the ill luck of some of her predecessors.

Two former holders of the name *Warspite*, now borne by one of our Polaris submarines, were destroyed by fire. The fifth *Vanguard*, built in 1787, was Nelson's flagship at the Battle of the Nile. But in 1875 the seventh holder of that name, an ironclad, was rammed and sunk by HMS *Iron Duke* while on exercises in the Irish Sea, and in 1917 her successor blew up in Scapa Flow with heavy loss of life. However, these calamities did not deter the Ships' Names Committee from choosing the name again for Britain's largest ever battleship, completed after the end of World War II and destined to be the last of her class. Yet it could be said by the superstitious that the baleful influence of the former hoodoo was still active, for this last representative of a splendid naval era was sent to the breaker's yard after only a few years in commission, and without ever having fired a shot in anger. As if protesting against her ignominious fate, she went aground in Portsmouth harbour at the start of her last journey and refused to budge for an hour.

A name with a shady past, which, however, had no effect on its re-use is *Adventure*, last conferred on a pre-World War II cruiser/minelayer. The fourth *Adventure* had been an armed merchantman hired in 1696 and commissioned for the suppression of piracy on the American coast and elsewhere by Captain William Kidd. But, acting presumably on the principle that 'if you can't beat 'em, join 'em', Kidd turned pirate himself. Yet there was honour also in the name. The first *Adventure*, built in 1594 at Deptford, took Drake and Hawkins on their last expedition to the West Indies; while the eighth was chosen by Captain Cook for his second voyage of discovery which lasted from 1772 to 1776.

Charles II introduced the 'Royal' system of nomenclature with such names as *Royal Charles, Royal James, Royal Prince, Royal Oak*, and the like. In 1665 the *Loyal London* was built for him with money subscribed by the City of London to replace the third *London* which had blown up in the Thames with the loss of nearly all on board. Unhappily the *Loyal London* was burnt by the Dutch when De Ruyter raided the Medway in June 1667. She was subsequently raised and repaired at the expense of the king who, because the City refused to provide the funds for this purpose, angrily cut off the prefix 'Loyal'. Thereafter her successors have been christened simply *London*. Today the present bearer of the name, a guided missile destroyer, maintains as did her predecessors a close liaison with the City of London and the Mercers' Company.

Naval names which formerly commemorated famous admirals have been extended in recent times to include those of distinguished captains, notably those who served with Nelson, and today are borne by a class of frigates. Territorial names as a fashion came in with the Commonwealth; others are of counties and towns, some of which reach back a long way in naval history. Today the names of many villages in the United Kingdom are borne by small mine countermeasures craft.

The names of insects and animals have also figured in the Navy List, together with classical and mythological names, although one wonders what the crew of HMS *Lacedaemonian* made of the pronunciation of that name in 1820, or, for that matter, HM ships *Terpsichore* and *Bucephalus*. Before the creation of the present-day Ships' Names Committee, eighteenth-century First Lords of the Admiralty frequently gave rein to their personal fancies, and one gentleman with sporting proclivities named a class of gun brigs after his pack of hounds – *Blazer, Boxer, Bruiser*, and so on, names which, incidentally, were revived in World War II for a number of tank landing ships. A class of bomb ketches were appropriately named *Etna, Beelzebub, Fury* and *Sulphur*. Abstract names such as *Dreadnought, Fearless* and *Intrepid* date back to Elizabethan times and live by tradition. Thus the first *Dreadnought* fought against the Armada; the eighth was famous as the first all-big gun battleship in 1906; while the latest to hold the name was launched in 1959 as Britain's first nuclear submarine.

Lengthy names are avoided where possible, since warship names must be able to appear on a sailor's cap ribbon. One such which went over the odds, however, was HMS *Weston-super-Mare*, known to her crew as the 'Aggie on Horseback' (a reference to the founder of the Sailors' Rests). The name eventually had to be shortened to HMS *Weston*. Another lengthy one was HMS *Emperor of India*, which of necessity had to appear in full. This is one particular warship name never likely to be used again.

Closely associated with the Ships' Names Committee is another body which considers and recommends the design of ships' badges and mottoes. Previously the Ships' Names Committee was in fact called the Ships' Badges Committee, but today they have become separate bodies, although membership is common to both. As well as the Head of the Naval Historical Library, it includes an officer of the College of Arms who is the adviser on naval heraldry.

Badges, or crests, have replaced the elaborate figureheads which once adorned the bows, or beakheads, of British warships of the past. In earlier times when much of the cost of building warships was met by the king, it was customary for the builder to include a good deal of ornamentation. The stern and quarter galleries were especially elaborately carved and gilded, this being described by the sailors as 'gingerbread work'. Damage to these in battle was

Ship's badge of H.M.S. *Orion*, flagship of Admiral Pridham-Wippell at the Battle of Matapan.

termed 'knocking the gilt off the gingerbread', and it is from this that the phrase in its present form derives. At the bows was the figurehead, usually symbolic of the ship or its associations. These figureheads were most popular with the sailors, who took great pride in keeping them in good repair with gilt and much bright paint. Born of a desire to beautify the ship and make her a living personality, figureheads were also great morale builders.

One of the British ships which took part in the Glorious First of June battle was the 74-gun *Brunswick*, whose figurehead was an effigy of the reigning duke in military uniform. Early in the action a shot struck off the carved wooden hat of the ducal figurehead. When the men working the forecastle guns noticed this disrespectful treatment of their ship's namesake, they asked their captain for one of his own gold-laced cocked hats to replace the missing headgear. This was duly produced, and, defying the hissing French bullets and cannonballs, some of the men clambered out on to the beakhead and nailed the hat in position!

For some years after the advent of ironclad warships, decorative scroll work and coats of arms were incorporated in the upper part of the stem of the vessel in place of the earlier figurehead. But with the changing bow shape of warships this form of decoration eventually disappeared, to be replaced by the present-day cast metal badge, which is usually secured to the front of the bridge structure. A replica of the badge is also carried on the bows of a warship's boats, reproduced on her gun tompions if she carries guns, and stamped on her official notepaper. Whatever the design, the badge is always surmounted by the naval crown formed of five alternate sails and sterns of ships. Known as the *Corona navalis*, this was originally awarded to the Roman heroes of sea fights. At first badges and mottoes were unofficial and often crude. In 1918 they were regularised by the Admiralty and the Ships' Badges Committee was formed.

The badges of two very different types of vessel in our existing fleet exemplify the work of the present day committee. Thus the crest of HMS *Egeria*, an inshore survey ship, consists of a lion's head with a stream of water flowing like a fountain. Egeria was a nymph of Aricia, in Italy, who was courted by Prince Numa and became his wife. When he died she was so grief-stricken that she could not stop weeping, and was changed into a fountain by Diana. The Royal Fleet Auxiliary *Fort Grange*, a 22,000-ton fleet replenishment ship, has on her crest the arms of Lord Palmerston, one of Queen Victoria's Ministers. She is named after one of a ring of forts encircling Portsmouth and Gosport which are referred to locally as 'Palmerston's Follies'. Built during that statesman's premiership, they were designed to protect the coast against an anticipated invasion by the French.

Below each ship's crest is an enscrolled motto, in the composition of which the Ships' Badges Committee and their heraldic adviser occasionally have to stretch their erudition in order to contrive a fitting Latin version. With the passage of time and the sailorman's humour, some of those which are borne by long established 'stone frigates' have acquired their own 'free' nautical translations. Thus the motto of HMS *Excellent*, the Navy's gunnery school,* which is *Si vis pacem para bellum* ('If you desire peace, prepare for war'), has long been interpreted as 'Attitude is the art of gunnery and whiskers make the man'. That of HMS *Vernon*, the Torpedo/Anti-

* Now known as the Naval General Training Centre.

Submarine School, is *Vernon semper veret* ('Vernon always flourishes' – the family motto of Admiral Vernon of 'grog' fame), but this has been transformed into 'Swing (leave) it till Monday', a libellous aspersion on the attitude of that establishment towards work!

Because of the large numbers of small vessels enrolled in the Navy during the Second World War, time did not permit of obtaining the approval of the Ships' Badges Committee for the many *ad hoc* crests and mottoes which adorned their bridges. Probably the simplest and most direct of these was that of HMS *Stella Rigel*, a former Hull fishing trawler turned anti-submarine vessel. Her company adopted for her crest a plain shield bearing the words, 'To Hell with Hitler!' An early *Artful* badge bore the appropriate design of a monkey 'proper'.

Intended to foster *esprit de corps* among officers and ships' companies along with crests and mottoes, and to encourage them to take a personal interest in the past exploits of their ships, is the award of battle honours to HM ships. Before the Second World War, battle honours were displayed in ships on the authority of their commanding officers. But in 1954 the Admiralty overhauled the whole system, and announced that from thenceforth they would be officially awarded by the Admiralty Board.

It was then decided that the earliest naval action of which sufficient is known, and in all respects worthy of inclusion is 'Armada 1588'. Actions and campaigns thereafter in which individual ships took part were to be displayed on a scroll mounted in a suitable position on board. In the past the tendency had been to regard battle honours in terms of naval history, and to include many actions and incidents which, though meritorious in themselves, were not of sufficient importance to be ranked as battle honours. Hereafter the new definition was to be an action which resulted in the defeat of the enemy, or where an engagement was inconclusive but well fought; and in exceptional circumstances where an outstanding effort had been made against overwhelming odds. A battle honour would not be awarded for a British defeat or an inconclusive action which had been badly fought. The new and revised list of fleet actions and campaigns for which battle honours were awarded numbered 165, ranging from the Armada to the Arctic convoys of 1941-45, and including such well known events as the First of June 1794, the Nile, Trafalgar, the Falkland Islands,

River Plate, Salerno, and the Normandy landings.

Battle honours on the new scale were awarded to existing ships of the post-war fleet, but today comparatively few of their names are to be found in the Navy List. All new holders, however, assume the appropriate battle honours of their predecessors as the names are re-used. The ship boasting the longest list of revised battle honours was HMS *Orion*, a 7,000-ton cruiser of the *Leander* class scrapped in 1949. Among the score awarded to her, dating from the Glorious First of June 1794, are Trafalgar, Jutland, Matapan, Malta convoys, Salerno and Normandy. So far no new ship of that name has joined the fleet of the seventies. But one famous name which is represented in the present-day fleet and is one of the oldest in British naval history, is *Swiftsure* (originally Swift-suer, i.e., pursuer) which can boast nineteen battle honours. Starting with the Armada, there have been holders of this name in the Royal Navy throughout the centuries, to the present *Swiftsure* which is, appropriately enough, a nuclear fleet submarine and the first of a new and modified class of these vessels.

For the first time in British naval history battle honours were awarded to Fleet Air Arm squadrons which, like ships, also have their own crests and mottoes. Of these No 820 Squadron can claim the most battle honours. They number eleven, and range from Norway in 1940 through to the defeat of Japan in 1945.

Whenever a new warship is commissioned which bears a name that has been used before, she also inherits along with the battle honours of her predecessors any plate and trophies which over the years have been presented to them. As ships are paid off for the last time these are landed for safe keeping in one or other of the royal dockyards to await a successor.

The practice of donating gifts to British warships by private individuals, their builders, civic bodies and other benefactors has been followed for a good many years. In earlier times great naval victories and other stirring sea fights were frequently recognised by the presentation of medals and plate to the commanders of victorious fleets and vessels, although not to individual ships themselves. Thus to commemorate the capture of Porto Bello by Admiral Vernon, he was presented with a gold box and the freedom of the city by the City of London. Admiral Charles Watson who, as Commander-in-Chief of the East Indies station, supported Clive in

King George III presenting a diamond-studded sword to Admiral Howe after the Glorious First of June Battle in 1744.

smashing French aspirations in India, was presented with a quantity of valuable jewels by the Prince of Hindustan. An exquisite Chinese miniature garden fashioned of coral, carved wood and ivory, mother of pearl, malachite and rose quartz was given to Commodore Anson during the latter's visit to the Canton river on his world voyage of 1740-41 by the Emperor Kien-lung. This is now preserved in the National Maritime Museum. Delighted at the victorious outcome of the Glorious First of June battle, George III went down to visit Admiral Howe's fleet at Spithead, presented the admiral with a diamond-studded sword, awarded medals and gold chains to certain of his officers, and gave two golden guineas to every man in the fleet.

It was the naming of warships after Dominions and Colonies, and counties, cities and towns in the United Kingdom which really started the fashion of presenting gifts to 'namesake' or 'adopted' ships. The whole thing might be said to have stemmed from the occasion when the city fathers of Plymouth presented Sir Francis Drake with a drum. Although intended as a personal gift, the drum always thereafter accompanied him to sea until his death in 1596.

In the heyday of the British Empire the Dominions, before they became independent nations and acquired navies of their own, and certain of the more wealthy colonies, were expected to help pay for the Empire's first line of defence by contributing funds towards the annual British naval estimates. These contributions, if particularly generous, were often recognised by conferring the name of the donating colony on a British warship, which was then 'adopted' by the former and made the recipient of valuable gifts of plate and trophies, either for decorative purposes in the officers' messes or to be competed for by their ships' companies, or both.

Probably the most lavish of such gifts made by a colony in comparatively recent times were those presented to the battleship *Malaya* by the peoples of the former Federated Malay States. In 1912 the latter offered the Imperial Government the gift of a first-class armoured ship. At that time the four *Queen Elizabeth* class battleships were about to be built, and HMS *Malaya* was the gratefully accepted fifth of the class. She and her consorts cost nearly £3 million apiece.

As the Fifth Battle Squadron of the Grand Fleet, the *Malaya* and her sisters were attached to Admiral Beatty's battle cruiser fleet, and all except the *Queen Elizabeth* took part in the Battle of Jutland. The *Malaya* was hit seven times and sustained more than a hundred killed and wounded. Proud of her part in the action, the peoples of the Federated Malay States began to take a closer interest in 'their' ship. Two months after Jutland she was presented on their behalf by the High Commissioner for the Straits Settlements with a ceremonial bell, into the molten metal of which a Malay silver dollar was thrown while it was being cast; and in the following year with a suit of silken ensigns, which included a Malay jack, fashioned by the European ladies of the Federated States. The

Malay jack was officially authorised by the Admiralty to be flown in battle and on special occasions. Subsequently generous sums of money were sent by the various States for the crew to buy themselves a film projector and other amenities, and also to provide a fund for the dependents of those killed at Jutland.

In 1920 approval was given for the battleship to visit the country of her origin. Amid scenes of the greatest enthusiasm the Rulers of the Federated States boarded the vessel and presented her with gifts, the value of which ran into many thousands of pounds. One of these was a huge elephant's tusk embellished with silver, which required two men to carry it, and contained the ceremonial address of welcome on vellum. Other gifts included gold and silver plate, carved models of tigers and elephants fashioned by expert native craftsmen from the finest wood and ivory, and an oil painting of the Ruler of the largest State executed by a world-famous artist. Normally the insurance on these gifts would have been prohibitive. When HMS *Malaya* was scrapped in 1948 her plate and trophies were taken into store; their future is uncertain, for it is unlikely that she will ever have a successor.

Valuable gifts were also made to several Tribal class destroyers built in 1938 just before the outbreak of World War II. HMS *Ashanti*, for example, was presented with a heavy shield made of solid 24-carat gold and an embossed silver bell by the Asantehene, chiefs and people of Ashanti. After a distinguished war career the *Ashanti* was scrapped in 1949. In 1956 the Admiralty loaned the shield and bell to the Gold Coast Regiment for display at Kumasi, Ashanti's capital, until required for a new vessel of the name.

The ninth *London* was presented in 1929 by the then Lord Mayor of London with the only picture gallery in the Navy, to be kept in trust for future ships of the name. The 'gallery' comprised 76 prints of previous *Londons* and the actions in which they took part, together with important views of the old city of London. Since there were too many to hang in the wardroom and captain's quarters, the surplus prints were distributed among various officers' cabins according to the specialisation of their occupants. Thus the Accountant (Supply) Officer was given a view of the Royal Mint, the Gunnery Officer the bombardment of Sebastopol, and so on.

Among the trophies in the present missile destroyer *London* is a humble coconut. It was presented to the ship by the Duke of

A Tribal Class frigate.

Edinburgh who, during a visit to the ship, watched the practice firing of her Seacat armament. Unerringly a missile sped to its target many thousands of feet up and scored a direct hit on a pilotless aircraft. 'The man deserves a coconut,' commented the Duke, praising the work of the Seacat aimer. No one thought any more about the remark until a few days later a parcel arrived from Buckingham Palace. In it with the Duke's compliments was a coconut. In accordance with the regulations this was duly registered as a ship's trophy.

HMS *Sussex*, a county class cruiser built in 1928, was presented with a salver inscribed with the names of all the captains of her predecessors back to 1690. In 1952 the city of Glasgow presented a silver wine server in the form of a model of a Spanish galleon to the cruiser *Glasgow* to cement ties established between the city and the ship in World War II. HMS *Gurkha*, a modern Tribal class frigate, which has fraternal links with the Gurkha Regiment, includes a ceremonial *kukri* among her trophies. When the weapon was presented, the commanding officer had his thumb pricked with it in acceptance of the tradition that a Gurkha never unsheaths the blade unless he draws blood.

Hanging in the captain's cabin of HMS *Eskimo*, another Tribal class frigate, is a magnificent Eskimo coat presented by the Hudson's Bay Company. This garment is worn by the commanding officer on ceremonial occasions, and when entering and leaving harbour. Centrepiece of the frigate's wardroom table is a model of an Eskimo *kayak* complete with rower in full detail, sculptured by an Eskimo out of a solid piece of granite.

HMS *Diamond*, one of a class of super destroyers built in the 1950s, was presented with many expensive tokens of goodwill by the famous firm of De Beers. These included a silver replica of the statue of Cecil Rhodes at Bulawayo, and a set of silver candelabra incorporating a diamond motif in the design. The officers of HMS *Duchess*, another vessel of the class, advertised in the press that they were anxious to hear from any duchess with a coronet to spare for their wardroom. Their appeal came to the notice of the Duchess of Westminster, who presented them with hers!

The aircraft carrier *Bulwark* includes among her presentation plate a ten and three-quarter inches high standing silver salt, believed to be the only one of its kind in the Royal Navy. Presented by the British Insurance Association to commemorate the part played by the carrier in the Suez operations of 1956, the salt has a domed cover supported by three heraldic seahawks signifying the three squadrons of Seahawk aircraft which took part in the operation.

The Fairfield Shipbuilding and Engineering Company, builders of the helicopter cruiser *Blake*, presented the ship with a splendid trophy in the form of a solid silver model of Admiral Blake's flagship, the *George*, on board which he died in 1657. Twelve inches long, the intricate stern galleries of the model were carved by hand from a solid block of silver. With rigging and spars fashioned of the same metal, the model took eight months to complete.

Over the years naval shore establishments, such as the naval barracks at the three home ports and the gunnery and torpedo schools, have been the recipients of large quantities of presentation plate and other gifts, ranging from heavy silver wine coolers and candelabra to ship models, boarding pikes, and paintings down to small silver ashtrays in the form of Victorian sailors' hats. The wardroom mess at Chatham barracks proudly displays among its collection of historic memorabilia a fascinating item of Nelsoniana. Written in the admiral's own handwriting and dated 13th September 1805, before he sailed from England for the last time, it is the original banker's order to Messrs Davison & Co., of Pall Mall, directing them to, 'Please pay on the first day of every month till further order to Lady Hamilton or order the sum of One Hundred Pounds'. The note is endorsed with a scrawled 'Emma Hamilton' and a cross.

CHAPTER IX

The Language of Flags

Once upon a time, before the Royal Navy's overseas stations were closed down in the 1950s and 1960s to disappear into the history books for ever along with the *Pax Britannica*, the commander-in-chief of one such station was about to relinquish his command at the expiration of his period of appointment in obedience to the traditional, sonorously worded directive from the Admiralty: 'You are to strike your flag and come on shore.' A local language newspaper reported that when the flagship turned over her duties to the relieving ship which was bringing out the new commander-in-chief from England, the two vessels would carry out a ceremony steeped in naval tradition. 'The ceremony', declared the paper's editor solemnly, 'will be marked by the firing of gun salutes and the simultaneous hoisting and lowering of the admirals in both ships'.

This was an event which the two flag officers must have been sorry to miss.

What the editor meant, of course, was that the *flag* of the retiring admiral would be simultaneously lowered with that of his successor being hoisted, thus ensuring continuity of command.

An admiral's flag is more than a mere symbol of rank. Not only are certain financial increments for himself and his staff dependent upon the continuity of its flying, but it confers the widest powers and responsibilities upon him, especially if he is a commander-in-chief. In battle his flag is worn boldly at the masthead and continues to fly even if he has been killed in the action.

In the early days of the Royal Navy the only personal flag flown afloat was the Royal Standard when the king took charge of his ships. Later, when the monarch ceased to go afloat, his personal standard was flown by the Lord High Admiral, as, for example, was done by Lord Howard of Effingham and not Sir Francis Drake, as is sometimes believed, who commanded the British fleet against the Armada. But in 1702 Queen Anne decreed that the Union Flag should be used as the distinguishing emblem of the Fleet's commander-in-chief, and today this has become the personal flag of an admiral of the fleet. Worn at the jackstaff, the Union Flag denotes a ship of the Royal Navy, and it is not allowed to be worn by any other ships. Only then should it properly be called the 'Union Jack'.

Normally officers holding this highest of naval ranks do not serve afloat, but during World War II it happened that Admiral Sir Charles Forbes, then Commander-in-Chief of the Home Fleet, was promoted admiral of the fleet on 8th May 1940. He was able to fly his Union Flag afloat until December of that year when he was relieved by Admiral Sir John Tovey. The announcement that an admiral of the fleet was actually serving afloat in wartime sent naval historians scurrying to the records in search of a precedent.

But the Lord High Admiral also had his own standard, a red flag with a golden (foul) anchor and cable (dubbed in consequence the 'sailor's disgrace'); and at one time this was flown over the building which housed his 'Council of the Sea'. The foul anchor badge was also used as a mark placed on ships and goods arrested by the Admiralty; also on naval ordnance. The flag was last flown afloat as his personal standard by HRH the Duke of Clarence, who for fifteen months held the revived office of Lord High Admiral, which had been first placed in commission by Charles I. In 1828 the Duke took a squadron of warships to sea for manoeuvres without seeking the approval of the Council which had taken over the administrative and executive duties of the Admiralty Board, much to the exasperation of the king. Following his resignation in August of that year, the office of Lord High Admiral was never again held by a single individual.

In 1850 the foul anchor flag was adopted by the Board of Admiralty, and flown night and day over the old Admiralty building in Whitehall until 31st March 1964 when the Board was absorbed into the newly created Ministry of Defence. It was then ceremonially hauled down for the last time, and the Queen herself assumed the title of Lord High Admiral. Whenever she officially goes afloat this flag, together with the Royal Standard and the Union Flag, is flown; the Royal Standard from the main, the Lord High Admiral's flag from the fore, and the Union Flag from the mizen masts, or in the most conspicuous parts of the ship.

In 1977 the Queen approved that the flag of the eighteenth-century Navy Office should be adopted as the flag of the Admiralty Board. This flag consists of three gold anchors, one large with a small one on either side, on a crimson ground. It is flown in ships and shore establishments when two or more members of the Admiralty Board, acting as a Board, are present, and displaces other flags of rank.

It is sometimes queried, even in naval circles, whether flags are 'worn' or 'flown' in ships. The answer is simple. For just as the old-time sailing warship was rigged out with a 'suit' of sails, so also was she provided – as are her modern counterparts – with a 'suit' of colours. These comprise a commissioning pennant, ensign and Jack. Thus when a warship flies an ensign or flag other than a signal flag she is said to be 'wearing' it. When on some special occasion, such as the Queen's birthday, she displays all her bunting on a line running from the ensign staff at the stern, over the mastheads and to the jackstaff forward, or 'dresses ship', she is said to be 'dressed overall'. In olden times standards and personal banners were hoisted, the standards of captured ships also being displayed as trophies. It follows, then, that an admiral flies his flag, but a ship wears it.

A warship's ensign which is not hoisted close up at the gaff or ensign staff gives a slovenly appearance to a ship, and would most certainly lead to the communications rating responsible 'stopping a bottle' (navalese for being reprimanded) for not doing his job properly. But adopting a slovenly appearance in one's person was also the ancient way of expressing grief. In Biblical times, for example, a grief-stricken person donned 'sackcloth and ashes'. This, then, is the origin of the custom observed today of a warship half-masting her ensign as a sign of mourning. Up to some seventy years ago, if the deceased had been a particularly prominent personage such as a king or president, the ship's yards would also be 'cockbilled' and lower booms drooped. It was the custom to 'cockbill', or dip, the foreyards to port and those on the mainmast to starboard. When the ensign was re-hoisted, all would be put right again by the order 'square away'.

It is customary for merchant vessels and yachts, whose masters and skippers know their etiquette, to dip their ensigns to a British warship, whether the latter be met at sea or passed in harbour. Not

British gunboats at Canton.

only is this an act of courtesy, it can also indicate that all is well on board the yacht or merchantman.

In pre-World War II days the Royal Navy maintained a couple of flotillas of gunboats on the now defunct China station. One day one of these gunboats arrived unexpectedly in a Treaty port to find a solitary British merchantman at anchor with no ensign flying. Hardly had the gunboat herself anchored than the merchantman hurriedly hoisted her Red Ensign – upside down – which she then proceeded to dip courteously before securing it in place, still the wrong way up. Observing this, the gunboat captain sent away his motorboat with armed sailors concealed below. When the boat came alongside the river steamer, a number of Chinese suddenly appeared on deck and began to throw themselves overboard. While some of the bluejackets swarmed on board the steamer, the rest stayed in the motorboat which sped off in pursuit of the swimming

Naval armed guard on their way to board a ship suspected to be in pirate hands.

Chinese; all the latter being recovered and hauled protestingly aboard. Meanwhile the sailors who had boarded the merchantman rounded up several more Chinese who, although armed, dropped their weapons and surrendered without a fight.

It transpired that the steamer had been attacked and taken over by pirates just before the warship's arrival. Her British chief engineer, however, managed to persuade his captors to allow him to hoist the ship's ensign under the pretext that the gunboat's captain would become suspicious if no ensign was flying. Guessing that the pirates would be unaware of its significance as a signal of distress, the chief engineer hoisted the ensign upside down, and the gunboat captain knew immediately that she was in trouble.

On one notable occasion in history, however, this ploy worked to our disadvantage. In 1801 the tiny gun brig *Speedy* which under the command of Captain Thomas Cochrane (later Admiral Lord Dundonald) had for fifteen months successfully raided French and Spanish shipping, was captured off Gibraltar by the French 74-gun *Dessaix*. Tackled by a British squadron, the *Dessaix*, with Cochrane

A typical up-river steamer. Although Chinese-owned, many were British registered and flew the Red Ensign.

a prisoner on board, and her consorts deliberately ran themselves ashore under the guns of their own batteries at Algeciras. HMS *Hannibal* followed them in to continue the fight, but herself ran aground, and after coming under heavy fire, was captured by the enemy.

On the French taking possession of the *Hannibal* they had neglected to provide themselves with their national ensign, and either from necessity or bravado rehoisted the English flag upside down. This being a well known signal of distress, was so understood by the authorities at Gibraltar, who, manning all government and other boats with dockyard artificers and seamen, sent them, as it was mistakenly considered, to the assistance of the *Hannibal*.

On the approach of the launches, I was summoned on deck by the captain of the *Dessaix*, who seemed doubtful what measures to adopt as regards the boats now approaching to board the *Hannibal*, and asked my opinion as to whether they would attempt to retake the ship. As there could be no doubt in my mind about the nature of their mission or its result, it was evident that if they were allowed to board, nothing could prevent the seizure of the whole. My advice to Captain Palliere was to warn them off by shot – hoping they would thereby be driven back and saved from capture. Captain Palliere seemed at first inclined to take the advice, but on reflection – either doubting its sincerity, or seeing the real state of the case – he decided to capture the whole by permitting them to board unmolested. Thus boat after boat was captured until all the artificers necessary for the repair of the British squadron, and nearly all the sailors at that time in Gibraltar, were taken prisoners!*

In sailing ship days it was the custom for merchantmen to strike or lower their topsails to British men-of-war. As mentioned in Chapter I, failure to do so could result in the pressing of some of the offender's prime seamen. The act of shortening sail was said to be 'in humble acknowledgment of his Majesty's Sovereignty of the British Seas and a grateful submission for their liberty to pass upon them'.

It was in fact the insistence of early English kings that English warships were to be saluted in the 'Narrow Seas' that sparked off the First Dutch War. Ships that failed to salute the English flag were fired on and even captured, and when in 1652 a squadron under Commodore Young fell in with a homeward bound convoy of Dutch merchantmen in the Channel he demanded of its senior officer the customary salute. When this was not forthcoming, the Dutch flagship was fired on and taken in prize.

This incident created great indignation in Holland. But while the diplomats of both countries were trying to smooth matters over, the Dutch naval commander-in-chief, Martin Tromp, who hated the English, appeared in the Downs with a powerful squadron of warships flaunting the Dutch colours. As expected, he encountered at the head of an English fleet Robert Blake, Cromwell's famous 'General-at-Sea', who demanded that the usual salute be given. When Tromp ignored his signal, Blake fired several warning rounds. The Dutch admiral's response was a shattering broadside into the English flagship. Battle was joined and the war was on. It

* *Autobiography of a Seaman*, Lord Dundonald.

ended in defeat for our opponents and Tromp's death.

When peace between our two nations was finally signed in 1654 the Dutch conceded our claim to the salute in home waters. But to this day regulations forbid the lowering of flags by British warships to any foreign ships whatsoever – unless the foreign ships shall first, or at the same time, lower their flags to them. This stems from regulations issued in 1806 which ordered that:

> Within his Majesty's Seas His ships are not on any account to strike their topsails, nor take in their Flags, nor in any way to salute any Foreign ship whatever; nor are they in any other seas to strike their Topsails, nor take in their Flags to any Foreign ships, unless such Foreign ships shall have first struck, or shall at the same time strike their Flags and Topsails to His Majesty's Ships.

And this in turn dated from 1734 when regulations for the Navy were first issued.

A happier reminder of earlier troubles with our Dutch neighbours is still extant and likely to be for many a year yet. Thus when Divine Service is being held on board a British warship, a special pennant consisting of a red St George's cross on a white ground with red, white and blue fly, is hoisted. Known as the 'Church pennant', this was first used around the year 1653 when our two countries first went to war with each other, and combines the flags of St George for England and the red, white and blue stripes of the Netherlands. Since both were Protestant nations, neither believed in fighting on Sundays, and the pennant was hoisted to indicate that the truce was in force.

One interesting ceremony which has become familiar to the British public through the medium of the annual Royal Tournament is that of 'Sunset', when the White Ensign in all naval ships and establishments is lowered at the close of day. The start of the Navy's official working day is also marked by a traditional ceremony known as 'Colours', the basic form of which has not changed for more than 170 years.

At a quarter to eight in the morning in summer and abroad, and nine in winter, a Royal Marine guard and band parades on the quarterdeck of every warship which carries a large enough marine detachment, and in every naval shore establishment where marines form part of the complement. Precisely at the hour, which is struck on the ship's bell, the bugler sounds the 'Alert', the guard presents arms, and the band plays the National Anthem as the White Ensign is slowly run up the ensign staff. Every person on deck, or who happens to be outdoors in a shore establishment, must face in the direction of the ensign staff, stand to attention and salute. In ships which do not carry either marines or a bugler, the quartermaster substitutes with appropriate blasts on the boatswain's call. During the ceremony all work and noise must cease. Power boats under way in a harbour or anchorage stop engines; pulling boats toss or lay on oars; sailing boats let fly sheets; crews come to attention, and coxswains salute.

If foreign warships are present in a British port or anchorage, such as Spithead, the national anthems of their countries are played after our own and in order of seniority of their flag officers, or in an order of precedence varied each day. When a British warship is visiting a foreign port, the national anthem of the country of that port is played after our own. When warships of a number of nations are present together with our own at an event such as the Coronation Naval Review held at Spithead in 1953, when the normal requirements of protocol would take too long to observe, only the national anthems of such foreign warships as are in the immediate vicinity of each British vessel are played, according to arrangements made beforehand.

In the days of Queen Elizabeth I there was no set routine for the daily hoisting of colours in British warships except when in harbour. Since there were then no Royal Marines, there was no martial music, and a seaman had to clamber aloft to the masthead to break out the appropriate flags required to be flown. In the seventeenth century colours were hoisted at sunrise and lowered at sunset to the beat of drum.

It was Admiral the Earl of St Vincent who, in 1800, as one of a number of measures for improving the discipline of the Channel Fleet, put the whole thing on a regular footing when he issued the following order from his flagship *Ville de Paris* at sea off Ushant where he was blockading the French. The first section of the order refers, as an awful example, to the loss of the *Royal Charles*, Howe's flagship at the Glorious First of June battle, which had been accidentally destroyed by fire with nearly 700 deaths:

For the maintenance of order and the preservation of His Majesty's Ships of the Line from fire and the dreadful calamities incident thereto, the following regulations are henceforth to be strictly observed when all or any of them are moored or at single anchor in Torbay, Spithead, Cawsand Bay, Portland Roads, or in any other bay or roadstead in Great Britain, Ireland, at Gibraltar, in Port Mahon (Minorca) and the Tagus, and on the coasts of France, Spain, Portugal, Italy and Bombay.

I

Guard to be paraded on the poop every morning at half past eight o'clock, with the form and order practised on the best regulated parades, and after going through a short exercise to descend to the quarterdeck at nine o'clock precisely, where all the accustomed formalities are to be gone through, with the respect or decorum due to the occasion, and, where there is a band of musick, after the Troop 'God Save the King' is to be played while the guard is under presented arms, and all persons present are required to stand with their hats off until the guard shoulders and after the Commanding Officer of the Detachment has received his orders from the Captain or Commanding Sea Officer on the quarterdeck, the arms to be lodged, and the guard held in constant readiness for occasional service.

Forty years later the time of the 'Colours' ceremony was altered to 0800 from 25th March to 20th September, or, roughly from the Vernal Equinox to the Autumnal Equinox; and 0900 from 21st September to 24th March. But colours can also be hoisted outside these hours in ships under way if there is sufficient light, and whenever British or foreign men-of-war enter or leave an anchorage. In action two ensigns are always displayed in a conspicuous position where they cannot interfere with signalling. This is done to ensure that there is always an ensign flying clearly visible to the enemy as well as to our own forces. If either should be shot away, a third is kept ready to be instantly broken out.

It has long been the custom for the ensign of any captured ship to be hoisted inferior (below) that of the flag of the captor. In the old days when an enemy ship desired to surrender, she hoisted the flag of her opponent superior to (above) her own.

When, as mentioned earlier in this chapter, British gunboats patrolled the rivers of China in the role of anti-piracy policemen, the senior officer of the West River Flotilla, whose ship was anchored off the city of Canton, observed one day to his angry astonishment that the greater part of a Red Ensign had been sewn into the rainbow patchwork of odds and ends which formed the mainsail of a passing Chinese junk. His indignation mounted further when his nostrils informed him that the vessel was engaged in the lowly business of removing the city's night soil.

At once he ordered away an armed motorboat, which pursued and overhauled the offending junk. The gunboatmen unceremoniously hauled down the sail, ripped out the fragment of the British flag, and brought the junkmaster back to the warship under arrest. There the trembling Chinese was kept on deck under the watchful eye of a massive bluejacket armed with rifle and bayonet until his relatives hastened on board to pay the fifty dollar fine the senior officer had summarily inflicted.

And in case it should appear that this action was pretty high-handed and not in the best interests of Sino-British relations, it must be pointed out that British naval officers on full pay have the right – in fact the duty – to seize any British ensign which is flown by an unauthorised person afloat. The flag so confiscated is forfeited to the Crown, and in addition the delinquent can be heavily fined. The Americans are even more severe about any misuse of the Stars and Stripes.

From about 1626 the fleets of the Royal Navy were divided into Red, White and Blue Squadrons. By the middle of the century ships belonging to these squadrons wore Red, White or Blue Ensigns as their distinguishing colours. The order of precedence was red, white and blue, although the squadrons took station respectively in the centre, van and rear of the Fleet. The promotion of admirals was then effected through these grades, Red being the senior. At Trafalgar, contrary to popular belief, Nelson was not a full admiral, but held the rank of vice-admiral of the White.

Squadronal colours were abolished in 1864, when the White Ensign was authorised to be worn by all ships of the Royal Navy, the Red Ensign by merchant ships, and the Blue Ensign by ships belonging to public offices, ships of the Colonial navies, and certain merchant vessels commanded by Royal Naval Reserve officers.

Senior Naval Officer, West River Flotilla about to pay an official call in his motor sampan with pennant flying.

Vessels belonging to the Royal Yacht Squadron are also allowed by Warrant to wear the White Ensign; many other yacht clubs wear the Blue Ensign with the club badge or crest in the fly. This general allocation of ensigns has remained in force ever since, but certain alterations in detail have been made from time to time by Acts of Parliament. Commonwealth navies, for example, now wear their own Jacks and naval ensigns.

Years ago according to legend when a warship was due to pay off at the end of her commission it was the custom of the ship's company to knot together all their brightwork cleaning rags and hoist them at the main truck as a sign that they were no longer required. Subsequently a long white pennant with a red St George's cross in the hoist took the place of the cleaning rags. This pennant was specially made on board, and custom ordained that every member of the ship's company should put in a few stitches.

Then the tradition grew that when a ship exceeded the normal period of her commission her paying-off pennant should indicate the extent of this spell of enforced overtime. Accordingly the length

H.M.S. *Birmingham* leaving the Cape of Good Hope station in the 1920s with her paying-off pennant flying.

of the pennant was fixed at the length of the ship herself for the correct paying-off date, with one-twelfth of this measurement added for 'every two months by which the normal commission period was exceeded. To prevent this outsize pennant from trailing in the water when hoisted at the masthead, a gilded pig's bladder was fastened to its extremity.

A more romantic story associated with the paying-off pennant is that it was intended to blow a ship homeward. Although in the main religious folk with a simple faith in the Almighty purpose, old-time sailors were nevertheless credulous and superstitious. In an early play about the sea it is mentioned:

> *Witches for gold will sell a man a wind,*
> *Which in the corner of a napkin wrapp'd*
> *Shall blow him safe unto what coast he will.*

There were always people to sell the sailors winds, and clergymen as well as witches and wizards were supposed to possess this valuable privilege. There is a story in most of the old collections of voyages of how a certain mariner purchased a selection of winds from a witch on the coast of Finland. The winds were contained in three knots tied in a rag, which rag was to be fastened to the mast, and the knots untied as the winds were required. The first two unloosed suited the sailors exactly and blew the ship homeward at a fine rate, but the third was a hurricane, so furious that the poor sailors thought God had sent it to punish them for their dealings with the Infernal One instead of trusting to His providence. Fortunately they possessed another charm which presently mitigated the force of the gale, and they arrived home safely. Macbeth's witches were able to give away winds, drawn from all the quarters 'that they may know i' the shipman's card', that is to say, from all points marked on the compass.*

Whatever its true origin, traditionally the paying-off pennant could only be hauled down on the actual day of paying off by the cook, who, at one time, ranked as a 'standing officer'. Says the *Naval Chronicle* for 1815:

> According to an established form in the Navy, when a ship is paid off no officer must quit the port or consider himself discharged until the pennant is struck; which can only be done by the cook as the last office at sunset; and should he be absent no other person can perform the office, however desirous the officers may be of taking their departure, and although there may not be a single seaman or Royal Marine on board.

With all the Christmas tree-like assortment of radar antennae, wireless aerials and the terminals of other electronic gadgetry which festoons the masts of modern warships, it would probably be a matter of some difficulty today to continue to follow the old custom of hoisting a garland on the wedding day of an officer belonging to a warship. Usually hoisted between the fore and mainmasts, the garland consists of two loops of evergreen, one inside the other at right angles to give the appearance of a sphere, with white silken streamers hanging down from the bottom.

* *The British Tar in Fact and Fiction*, Robinson.

This custom had its origin in the days of sailing warships when wives and sweethearts were allowed on board a vessel returning from sea. For the first two or three days in port very little work was done, and the garland was hoisted to indicate that the ship was 'out of routine' and need not be visited by the Officer of the Guard. After the wedding garland has been hauled down, it is customary for it to be left in the bridegroom's cabin for him to find on return from his honeymoon. On Christmas Day it is the custom to display a sprig of holly at the trucks and yardarms.

A welcome signal still flown today when a warship wishes to celebrate a special occasion is a single green and white pennant. Known as the 'Gin Pennant', this is an open invitation to one and all to come and join the party, for a gin-drinking session is about to take place.

Certain other admirably terse signals are in use in the Navy to cover various official and social occasions. Thus the letters 'R.P.C.' mean 'Request the pleasure of your company at ...'; to which, if the invitation can be accepted, the reply would be either 'W.M.P.' (With much pleasure), or 'V.M.T.' (Very many thanks). On the other hand, if it must be declined, 'M.R.U.' (Much regret I am unable to) would have to be signalled; or, if initiator and addressee are on sufficiently familiar terms with each other, even 'N.C.D.' (Regret no can do). If transport is required, the appropriate signalled request is 'P.S.B.' (Please send boat), unless the initiator of the invitation has thoughtfully added the letters 'W.S.B.' (Will send boat at ...). The signal 'I.C.U.' means 'Can I come and see you at ...', while 'U.C.M.' means, 'Can you come and see me now, or (at time given)'.

CHAPTER X

Guardians of the Gangway

The scene was the gangway of a British naval headquarters ship lying off an enemy-held coast during World War II. The initial assault landing of the Allied invasion force was well under way, and the Army commander, an American general, was preparing to disembark to set up his command post on shore. Held with difficulty alongside the accommodation ladder of the vessel by her crew of two, a small, blunt-bowed landing craft tossed and plunged in the rough seas, for the weather had become unpleasantly boisterous.

Speeded on his way with a sketchy salute from the young and inexperienced quartermaster of the headquarters ship, the general apprehensively descended the ladder. After trying vainly to step over the heaving gunwale of the landing craft, the general finally abandoned the attempt and scrambled into it on all fours. Before he could regain his feet, his aides, who had followed him down the ladder, fell on top of him. Then, in an undignified welter of arms and legs, steel helmets, webbing gear, weapons and hand luggage, the general's boat shoved off for the shore.

If the officer of the watch of the headquarters ship had not been called away from his post at that particular time this lubberly scene would never have been allowed to be enacted. For it is an old and revered custom in the Royal Navy that a senior officer enters a boat last and disembarks from it first. The very good reason for this is, of course, that the VIP is thereby subjected to the least possible incommoding of his illustrious person or wetting by flying spray. Equally it is traditional that a junior officer enters a boat first and leaves it last.

It is related that once, long ago, when tempers afloat were far more choleric than they are ever likely to be today, two British warships bound on different missions whose captains were of like seniority shared the same temporary anchorage for the night. On the following morning Ship Number One began to weigh anchor preparatory to departing about her business. At once came a peremptory signal from Ship Number Two, the name of whose captain appeared in the Navy list before that of the captain of Ship Number One. 'You should ask my permission to proceed', it said.

The signal was, however, ignored, and Ship Number One continued with her preparations for sailing.

Then a second and more ominous signal was hoisted in Ship Number Two. 'Unless you ask my permission to proceed,' was the message spelt out by the flags, 'I will open fire on you!' And in earnest of this deadly threat her guns were seen to be trained upon Ship Number One.

Promptly a string of bunting climbed to the latter's yardarm. 'Request permission to proceed in execution of previous orders', the message begged humbly.

After a few minutes the guns of Ship Number Two were ostentatiously unloaded, and with slow dignity her signal flags rose in reply. 'You may proceed', read the message graciously.

Thus possible bloodshed was averted, ruffled feelings soothed, and an old Navy custom properly, if belatedly, observed. For by regulation a junior captain must always 'wait upon' his senior when two British warships meet in a port or anchorage – although his orders cannot be interfered with by the latter – and he must ask his senior's formal permission to proceed on parting company, even when both officers are of the same relative seniority. There can be no hair-splitting over this apparently knotty point, for the name of one of the two will always appear before that of the other in that nautical *Who's Who*, the Navy List; and by virtue of that fact he is thus the senior. When in company with another 'private ship', the latter must by regulation fly a senior officer's pennant.

It was that nautically minded monarch Henry VIII who first issued the order that no junior captain should 'take the wind of his admiral', or, in other words, cross to windward of the flagship and thus take the wind out of his sails. Thus, although the sailing warship has long become a thing of the past, we have the origin of the modern custom in the Navy of asking permission before steaming across the bows of a flagship (at a safe distance of course). Thereby, too, derives the well-known phrase about taking the wind out of his sails when one verbally deflates an opponent in an argument or otherwise nonplusses him.

Until comparatively recently whenever a warship entered or left harbour, long-standing regulations required that she should carry out hand soundings, notwithstanding that a captain might know perfectly well from his charts and his familiarity with a port the depth of water beneath his ship, and the existence of any possible hazards to stranding. Failure to observe this regulation, however, might well help to convict a captain unlucky enough to go aground while engaged in this manoeuvre at his subsequent court martial for hazarding his ship.

All ships were then fitted with two small hinged platforms, one at either side, placed forward of the bridge. Called the 'chains', from olden days when the mast shrouds were secured to platforms bearing that name outside the bulwarks, a seaman stood on each ready to heave his hand lead.

This consisted of a leaden plummet weighing about 14 lbs, shaped like a policeman's truncheon, with a cavity at the base forming a cup. 'Armed', or filled with tallow, the purpose of this was to pick up a sample of the sea bed. Spliced to an eye at the top of the lead was the leadline, consisting of some twenty-five fathoms of specially woven 1-inch rope. The rope was marked along its length with two strips of leather at two fathoms; three strips at three fathoms; and one piece of leather with a hole in it at ten fathoms. Five and fifteen fathoms were marked by a strip of white duck; seven and seventeen with red bunting; thirteen by a strip of blue serge; and twenty fathoms by two knots. If, after being hove, the leadline should cut the water at any intervening fathom, this was known as a 'deep'.

To commence sounding, the sailor held the lead on a short length of rope in his outboard hand, left or right depending on whether he stood in the port or starboard chains, with the remainder of the line neatly coiled in the other. Leaning outboard and restrained only by a waist-high canvas apron, he then swung the lead to and fro until sufficient momentum had been obtained, when a sharp jerk of the wrist brought it flying over his head. Known as 'flying the blue pigeon', three complete circles usually sufficed to ensure that when released the lead would enter the water far enough ahead for it to sink to the sea bottom and enable the slack of the rope to be gathered in until the line was straight up and down by the time the slowly moving ship had reached that point. The mark, or 'deep',

Heaving the lead.

whichever it was, would then be noted, and the leadsman sang this out; for example, 'By the mark seven' for seven fathoms, or 'Deep nine' for nine fathoms. Soundings continued to be taken in this fashion until the ship had either reached the harbour entrance if outward bound, or was approaching the jetty if coming alongside from sea.

With the introduction of more sophisticated depth-finding devices, however, hand sounding is rarely used today, except by hydrographic ships when checking water depths close inshore for the purpose of chart-making. Charts, which are to the mariner what road maps are to the motorist, indicate *inter alia* not only depth of water but also the nature of the sea bed, whether rock, clay, sand or shingle. Hence the necessity for 'arming' the lead, since the sample thus obtained can be checked with the chart marking in any particular area.

In the old days before the invention of mechanical sounding machines, depth-taking at sea was a troublesome, lengthy and not always reliable business. When it was about to be undertaken, sailors were stationed at intervals along the chains, the foremost holding the lead itself, to which were attached many hundreds of feet of rope bearing fathom-indicating marks. Each man held a coil of the rope in his arm ready to cast it overboard when his turn came. The ship would be stopped, and at a given signal the first man hove the lead overboard, singing out, 'Watch, there, watch!' As it vanished below the water and its pull was felt, the others would cast off their coils in succession, repeating the warning cry until the lead finally reached bottom. The mark on the rope nearest to the point at which it cut the water was then noted, and the laborious task begun of hauling the whole contraption inboard again.

In those days a romantic custom was frequently followed in ships returning from foreign parts. Thus when the lead was first hove in English waters, an officer carefully removed the particles of sand and grit adhering to the tallow at the bottom of the lead, dropped them into a glass of wine, swilled them round, and drank the toast, 'Happiness and prosperity to our native land'. The same particles, which he was at pains not to swallow, were then sent forward to be dropped into the men's grog tub so that all could participate in the toast. But of course, there were no short foreign commissions in those days. After spending anything up to ten years or more overseas, the old-time man-o'warsman returning home would probably have been glad to chew a lump of his native soil as well as drink some of the stuff.

If a sailor's eye happens to light on a shipmate's pin-up of some curvaceous 'dolly bird', he might well fervently exclaim that he would like nothing better than to present the young lady with his 'black bag'. This is a genuine bit of old Navy, for the mariner of yore did indeed possess a black bag. This article was in fact a small holdall that either he or a nimble-fingered shipmate had run up from a spare piece of sailcloth, or similar material, and painted black in the same way as he did his tarpaulin hat. In it he kept his most precious personal possessions, including his best shore-going rig. To present this bag to a lady was tantamount to an offer of marriage.

In 1870, however, a small chest known as a 'ditty box' was introduced for seamen in which to keep their private papers and other odds and ends. Strongly constructed of white wood with a lock and brass name plate, the ditty box measured twelve inches by six by eight inches. Inside its lid the sailor generally kept photographs of his wife and family, if he had one, or his girl if he hoped to have one. Accordingly the black bag disappeared, but the saying lives on. The ditty box itself ceased to be a Navy issue in 1938.

No one knows quite why it was called by that name, but there are several possible origins. One is that 'ditty' came from the Saxon word *dite*, meaning neat and tidy. Another is that the box was the right size for holding the 'ditties', 'quid-ditties' and 'odd-ditties', which were pamphlets or squibs with a popular naval flavour frequently published during the eighteenth and nineteenth centuries. A third is that its forerunner, the black bag, was generally made of 'dittis', said to be a variety of Manchester cotton. Certainly mention of 'ditty bags' frequently crops up in old books about the Navy.

Up to the 1920s a large blue checkered handkerchief was included in a seaman's official kit. It was chiefly intended for use as a luggage carrier when he went on leave, in which to bundle up his spare clothing, clean underwear, toilet articles, etc., and any curios or other presents he might have purchased abroad for his family and friends. Thus the sailor of Victorian and Edwardian times coming ashore on leave was usually pictured as a faintly comic character clutching his bundle in one hand and, often, a parrot cage in the other. But to be dubbed a 'bundle man' by his shipmates meant that a sailor was married, since he seldom went ashore in his home port without carrying a bulging bundle handkerchief, which usually contained dirty linen for his spouse to wash. When sailors began to carry attaché cases instead of the despised bundle handkerchief, the latter ceased to be issued, and the cases were officially approved as an article of kit.

Sailors were ever leg-pullers, and few new entries joining their first seagoing ship escape an invitation to view the spot 'where the dead Marine was buried'. In the old French 'wooden walls' such a macabre visit might well have been possible, for the French were believed to bury men slain in action in the ship's ballast. The British Navy, although not then particularly noted for hygiene, preferred a cleaner resting place for those of their shipmates killed in battle. Their corpses were unceremoniously thrown overboard – marines included.

In more recent times the bodies of sailors killed in action were sewn up in their hammocks with a weight at head and foot, and launched over the side after a brief religious service. When this was done during the First World War, it was customary to thread the last stitch through the nose of the deceased. The reason was to remove any possibility of putting a body overboard while in a state of catelepsy, the shock of having a stitch passed through the nose with a sailmaker's needle being considered sufficient to bring the 'dead man' back to life. It was also customary for many years for the man who sewed up the corpse, usually the sailmaker, to be paid a guinea a body.

While serving as First Lieutenant of HMS *Legion*, we had occasion to bury three dead Germans, and I remember that my upper deck petty officer did his best to cajole three guineas out of me, but was met with the remark that I had no cash to spare for live Boches and certainly did not propose to chuck any away on dead ones, and that he had better make an official request through the captain. The above-mentioned Boches were killed in the action (of light forces of the Harwich Flotilla with four German destroyers off the Dutch coast) of 17th October 1914.*

Since the deliberate propagation of the disease myxomatosis some years ago, the rabbit population of Britain has been greatly reduced. But the naval version is still going strong. For the unofficial definition of this nautical animal is 'anything made on board ship from Service stores with the object of landing it for one's own use'. No one knows how the term started, but it may well have originated at Chatham in the days when St Mary's Island, now part of the naval dockyard, was inhabited by large colonies of *lepus cunicula*. Since the island was Admiralty property the removal of any rabbit was regarded as poaching. Nevertheless the sailor was as fond of a bit of rabbit pie as anyone, and numbers of rabbits concealed in kitbags and other forms of luggage used to find their way out of the dockyard. Hence the warning cry sometimes heard today when a sailor is going on leave with a bulging suitcase of, 'Tuck its ears in!'

On one particular foreign station beloved of the Navy back in the great days of Empire, the native tradesmen pursued a trustful custom of not demanding immediate payment in cash for goods and services supplied to naval men. 'Just sign chit, sah', they would grin invitingly, and weaker men did. Periodically, however, came the day of reckoning, and those who had taken full advantage of this insidious system of 'live now, pay later' frequently found themselves confronted with an awesome pile of chits they had thoughtlessly signed, which knocked the stuffing out of their pay packets. Many volunteered to serve for a further period on the station – not to settle down, but to settle up!

There were some naughty ones, however, who succeeded in eluding their clamorous creditors until their ship was safely homeward bound with the paying-off pennant streaming. 'First turn of the screw (propeller)', they would chortle jubilantly as they saw the shoreline and the angry, fist-waving tradesmen receding, 'pays all debts'. In this they were merely echoing an age-old sentiment, expressed in slightly different words by their tarry-breeched predecessors, who in similar case declared that they had 'paid all debts with the topsail sheet'. Just an old – and reprehensible – naval custom!

* *A Few Naval Customs, Expressions, Traditions & Superstitions*, Beckett.

As a military encampment must be guarded by sentries, so must a fleet anchorage station watchers for a similar purpose, for in peacetime warships do not need to shelter in heavily fortified harbours, but frequently anchor in comparatively open waters. In wartime a variety of sophisticated devices can detect the approach of air, surface and underwater intruders, supplemented by a large number of trained lookouts. Although certain of these devices are operated in peacetime, the ship's watchers are usually reduced to the gangway staff, who consist of the officer of the watch, quartermaster, boatswain's mate (who may combine both duties) and, if a marine detachment is carried, one marine to act as 'Corporal of the Gangway'. This handful of individuals, who work in watches right round the clock at sea and in harbour, is more than enough in normal times to detect and report the approach of another vessel, from a fleet replenishment ship to a Gemini dinghy and, as it were, to carry out the combined duties of sentry, doorkeeper and night-watchmen.

In a fleet anchorage and naval port there is a standard challenge and answer system just as there is on shore, but with a difference. The naval system, which is traditional, enables the gangway staff to determine the rank and identity of a visitor while his boat is still a comparatively long way off and to make adequate preparations for his proper reception. The challenge, which is unchanging, consists of the words 'Boat ahoy!' shouted either through a megaphone or a loud-hailer. The word 'ahoy' is not pronounced syllabically in the meticulous manner of a BBC announcer with accent on the aitch, but is deliberately slurred so that the challenge sounds like 'Boat-oy-y!' The reason is that, delivered in this manner, the hail will carry clearly over the sound of wind and rain and the noise of engines.

On being hailed the coxswains of all naval craft must respond at once, but their replies vary according to the identity of any passengers carried. Thus the coxswain of a boat having the Sovereign or any member of the Royal Family on board approaching a warship at night in a fleet anchorage would reply, 'Standard', signifying the Royal Standard which would be flying in the boat by day. Even if the royal personage is known to be paying a visit to the Fleet and is merely making a routine and well-advertised journey across the harbour, the boat must still be hailed and the reply given in the traditional manner. Not only the ship being honoured with a visit by royalty, but also every other warship passed en route at night must still hail the royal barge. But to each of their hails, except that of the ship for which he is bound, the coxswain replies, 'Passing'. By day of course, such challenges would be unnecessary since the Royal Standard would be clearly visible.

If the Admiralty Board, or any members of it on official duty, should be afloat in a harbour or fleet anchorage at night, the coxswain of this craft replies to the challenge the one word, 'Admiralty'. By day a replica of the Board's flag would be flying in the boat.

A commander-in-chief or other admiral afloat in his barge at night shows no special distinguishing lights, and his craft must be hailed like any other. The reply of the admiral's coxswain to the challenge is 'Flag', followed by the name of the flagship, for in a large assembly of warships there may be more than one admiral present. If the boat is not carrying the admiral himself but his chief of staff or captain of the fleet, the coxswain answers the hail with the word 'Staff', followed by the name of the staff officer's ship.

The coxswain of a boat carrying a warship's captain replies to the hail of the ship he is approaching with merely the name of the captain's command. If the passengers are officers, other than the captain, the reply to the hail is 'Aye, aye', but if there are no officers in the boat at all, the reply is 'No, no', and this reply is given even though a passenger may be on board in the person of a Cabinet Minister or the Archbishop of Canterbury. Since, however, no such distinguished passenger would be subjected to the discourtesy of having to embark in a warship's boat without being received on the jetty, or at the embarkation point, by an emissary of appropriate rank to escort him to the ship, it is likely that the reply in all such cases would be 'Aye, aye'.

As shown by the following, routine has changed but little over the years.

It has been a custom in the Service ever since we had a regular navy, for the sentinel on the gangways to challenge all boats approaching the ship at night. This is done first with a view to prevent surprise and ensure the vigilance of the watch, and next to ascertain the rank of the officer who may be coming alongside. The latter object is effected in so strange a manner, and in a language which to the uninitiated may appear to partake so closely of the nature of a secret cypher that its notice may with strict propiety be introduced under the present head of Naval Anomalies.

In the first instance the challenge thus comes from the sentinel, 'Boat ahoy!' – if it be a captain the answer will be the name of the ship he commands; by this technicality his rank is immediately recognised and preparation for his reception is made accordingly. If it be a lieutenant, the answer to the hail will be 'Holloa!' The sentinel then says, 'Coming here?' – the reply from the boat will be 'Aye, aye'. This at once denotes *his* rank; but, strange to say, in the case of a midshipman, his reply to the first challenge is uniformly, though most inexplicably, given in the negative, 'No, no!' All doubts are however cleared by the answer to the second interrogatory, 'Coming here?' – which is in the affirmative, 'Yes'.*

The nocturnal watchfulness of the Fleet is not left entirely to individual ships. Gangway staffs are, after all, only human, and it may occasionally happen that the deck is left untended for short periods. In foreign waters thefts from the deck, and even from cabins below decks, are not uncommon. Whenever a squadron of warships is anchored together, therefore, one vessel daily is usually detailed to act as 'guardship'. This function entails such odd duties as collecting and distributing mail to the assembled ships, providing a medical officer at short notice, and receiving and relaying routine wireless messages.

Not least of the duties of the guardship is to send one of her boats in charge of an officer round the anchored ships at unannounced times during the dark hours. This craft prowls quietly up and down the anchorage, keeping a lookout for unauthorised vessels which may be hanging about, or for any other untoward occurrence which appears to require investigation. Most important, the officer of the guard is keenly on the alert to see that his boat is promptly and properly hailed. If it can creep alongside unchallenged, he can board the offending ship to discover the reason. There have been

---

* *The Naval Sketch Book*, Captain W.N. Glascock, RN, 1826.

cases in the past when an officer of the guard has managed to slip on board a vessel unobserved and undetected and, seeing no one about, has made off with the rough deck log, involving the subsequent carpeting of the guilty officer of the watch next day. The reply of the officer of the guard to a warship's hail is, 'Guard boat'.

Another duty of the fleet guardship is that of boarding an incoming foreign man-of-war. The officer of the guard dons full dress with sword for his visit, and his boat flies a special pennant. Years ago every warship maintained a special pulling boat for such occasions as well as for the captain's personal use. This was either a gig or a galley, carvel built, splendidly painted, and kept scrubbed and polished to a state of almost unnatural cleanliness. Each man in her crew was hand-picked and a first-class seaman. To behold one of these craft going about her official business, with paintwork gleaming, long polished oars flashing in and out of the water in perfect co-ordination, their shining blades meticulously feathered at every stroke, made an impressive picture of nautical smartness and efficiency.

Today they have been replaced by fast motorboats for official duties, but a good boat's crew can still invest their work with something of the old-time *panache*. When coming alongside, for instance, bow and sternsheetmen bend together to pick up their boathooks, hold them out at arm's length across their chests for a moment, and then stand with them erect with the perfect timing of guardsmen presenting arms.

By day challenges are unnecessary except in thick weather, for the Fleet's boats when engaged on important duties exhibit certain distinguishing marks to enable gangway staffs to tell at a glance the identity or business of their occupants. Thus a commander-in-chief's barge, when carrying the Great Man on official journeys, wears prominently in the bows the appropriate flag to which he is entitled. As a senior flag officer is on ceremonial occasions entitled to be saluted by a Royal Marine guard and band, even though he may be only passing, he gives everyone plenty of time to prepare by signalling beforehand that he will be 'afloat with his flag flying'. Admirals' barges, however, also carry metal discs on which are painted the colours of the 'Affirmative' and 'Negative' flags. Thus the 'Affirmative' means, 'Yes, the Old Man is aboard', and the

'Negative' signifies, 'Don't panic – we have left him behind!' The fleet mail-boat exhibits a checkered disc in the bows. The boat containing the commanding officer of a warship, however minor, afloat on official business flies a long slender pennant bearing a red St George's cross. But no special salute is accorded to him by any ship save the one he is visiting.

CHAPTER XI

'To whistle a welcome'

One of the most historic and fascinating Navy customs is that of 'piping the side' when a distinguished visitor boards a British warship; not, it should be stressed, just any old 'distinguished visitor'. This is a purely naval salute reserved for the Queen, the Duke of Edinburgh when in naval uniform, members of the Royal Family of the rank of naval captain, or R.N. Reserve, when in naval uniform; members of the Admiralty Board when acting as a Board, and naval members when in uniform; Commonwealth Naval Boards when acting as Boards; flag officers and commodores in uniform; all foreign naval executive officers, the commanding officers of HM Ships, no matter how junior in rank; the Officer of the Guard or any naval officer flying a pennant and representing his captain; the president of a court martial, and the corpse of an officer or sailor.

Viceroys, civil governors, military officers, whether foreign or otherwise, consular officers and civilians, no matter how eminent the latter may be, are not entitled to this form of salute.* And it is only given between the hours of 'Colours' and 'Sunset', except for foreign naval officers who are piped on board at all hours.

In former times piping the side was not only a mark of respect: it was also used for hoisting the VIP bodily in or out of the ship by means of a yardarm whip and boatswain's chair when the ship was at sea. In the days of sailing warships, captains were frequently summoned on board the flagship to attend councils of war held by the admiral, or to receive special orders from him, while the Fleet was at sea and the weather too rough to permit the use of the sea

---

* At the State funeral of the late Sir Winston Churchill in 1965, his coffin was ceremonially piped by the Royal Navy on board the Port of London Authority launch at Tower Pier which took it up river, and again on disembarkation at the Festival Pier for conveyance to Waterloo Station – an unprecedented honour for a civilian.

gangway. As the latter consisted merely of horizontal treads in the ship's side, boarding was difficult from a small boat plunging alongside. The officers were therefore hoisted in and out.

In more recent times such a transfer was made by a flag officer at sea in 1942 when Rear-Admiral Robert Burnett, escorting Convoy QP 14 homeward from Russia, shifted his flag from the cruiser *Scylla* to the destroyer *Milne*. On that occasion the admiral, who was somewhat on the portly side, used an armchair with a metal frame and canvas seat, and was hoisted out by the *Scylla*'s crane instead of the old-time boatswain's chair and yardarm whip.

The pipe is always sounded twice, the first being the old order 'Hoist' from boat to ship, and the second 'Lower away' from mid-air to deck. Sounded on their whistles, or 'Calls', by the quartermaster and his boatswain's mates, the pipe today is sounded as a VIP's boat is coming alongside and bow and sternsheetmen are standing with their boathooks up; and the second as the VIP ascends the gangway ladder and enters the ship. Even today the officer of the watch in a warship may give the order 'Hoist him in', meaning to start piping. And should the distinguished visitor arrive by helicopter or motor-car, the reception procedure remains basically the same.

Should an officer or rating die or be killed on board ship and be taken ashore for burial, his body is ceremonially piped over the gangway on its last journey. Boats passing the vessel which is landing the corpse also salute in a variety of ways. Those under sail let fly the sheets, pulling boats toss their oars, and motorboats stop engines. Thus the Navy's highest honour is paid without distinction to the departed, admiral and seaman alike.

The use of the 'Boatswain's Call' – the correct name of the whistle employed – is almost lost in antiquity, but it is known that the galley slaves of ancient Greece and Rome kept stroke by the flute or whistle. Its use in English ships can be traced back to the days of the Crusades, when the crossbowmen were piped to come on deck and engage the enemy. It has always been used as a whistle of command and employed for passing orders, and blown as a salute to certain personages. Thus Captain Nathaniel Boteler in his *Dialogues* published in 1634 described the procedure for the reception of high personages on shipboard, which is very similar to that of the present time.

Notice therefore being given that upon such a day, the Prince himself, or his High Admiral of the Kingdoms, or some General of a present fleet, intendeth to visit any of his chief ships before they go out to sea; and that his pleasure is to be publicly, and with ceremony, received aboard. By the break of that day, the ship is in every part to be made neat and clean, and to be trimmed with all her ensigns and pendants; the ship's barge is early in the morning to be sent from the ship to the shore, perfectly furnished with carpets, cushions, tilt, and the like; the Coxswain with his whistle and best clothes being to attend in the stern, and the barge's gang in their liveries to row. And as soon as the Prince hath set his foot within the barge, the Standard Royal, or at least the flag, is to be let fly and to be fixed in the head of the barge; the which flag or standard is afterwards, at his coming aboard the ship, to be let fly, or heaved out in her main-top; and upon the first ken of the barge from the shore, the ship's decks, tops, yards and shrouds, are all to be thoroughly manned; and the shrouds to be (as it were) hung with men. Upon the more near approach of the barge, the ship's noise of trumpets (a set of four of different pitch) are to sound; and so to hold on until the barge come within less than musket shot of the ship. And then the trumpets are to cease; and all such as carry whistles are to whistle a welcome three several times; and in every interim the ship's whole company are to hail the barge with a joint shout, after the custom of the sea. As soon as the whistles and shouts of salute and welcome are stilled, the trumpets are again to sound a welcome to the ship's side. And that side, which is the port, or entering side, is to be very well manned with the primest and best fashioned men of the ship's company ready on both sides of the ladder. The Captain of the ship is upon the deck to present himself, just as the Prince enters, upon his knee, and so to receive him into the ship ...

Research farther back into history unearths continuous references to this instrument. Shakespeare makes mention of the 'master's whistle', as also do Ben Jonson and other early dramatists.

Probably owing to the fact that it has always been used as a method of passing orders, it was an honoured badge of rank, and in English ships and fleets as far back as the year 1485 it is known that it was the emblem of rank of the Lord High Admiral of England, at that date John De Vere, Earl of Oxford. It can also be traced as having been worn in action and used by Sir Edward Howard who, as Lord High Admiral, was killed in action with the Chevalier Prégent de Bidoux in 1513.

At that time England was at war with France, and Howard had crossed the Channel with forty-two sail to ravage the country around Brest. As part of their defensive measures the French had enlisted the services of a number of Maltese galleys, which were excellent fighting vessels, under de Bidoux, a knight of Malta. The English fleet discovered the galleys lying in Conquet Bay, whose waters were too shallow to permit their larger ships to enter.

Howard therefore transferred to one of his smaller vessels with some seventy men and grappled with de Bidoux's galley. After only seventeen Englishmen, with Howard at their head, had managed to scramble on board the enemy vessel, the two craft somehow drifted apart, and the French were able to overwhelm and kill their assailants. When Howard saw that his capture was imminent, he threw his gold Lord High Admiral's whistle into the sea. This action was commemorated movingly, if perhaps not strictly accurately, by the late Rear-Admiral Ronald Hopwood in his poem 'The Bosun's Call',* which runs:

> Lord Edward Howard walked his quarterdeck,
> His badge of Henry's royal hand bestowed,
> The golden call and chain about his neck,
> High Admiral of England.
>
> Up from the south, and who shall say him nay,
> Came the Chevalier Prégent de Bidoux,
> His fleet of galleys formed in brave array,
> Off Brest, across the Channel.
>
> 'But six ships we, Your Lordship, few and small',
> 'The better, then, my whistle ye shall hear',
> 'And rally to the watchword in its call',
> High Admiral of England.

* From his book *The Old Way*, John Murray (Publishers Ltd, 1916).

So forth they fared, by oar and wind and tide,
Faithful to follow where my Lord should lead,
His galleys laid along the foeman's side,
Off Brest, across the Channel.

He called his boarders. Swift they made reply,
'St George for England', leaping from the decks,
And ever in the van his battle cry,
High Admiral of England.

While yet they swarm across, nor count the cost,
The galleys drave asunder, leaving there
Him and sixteen to face de Bidoux's host,
Off Brest, across the Channel.

To fight and die unyielding in their prime,
A hundred swords and pikemen thrust them down,
And last was he borne fighting over side,
High Admiral of England.

Who, scorning death so that his honour be
All pure, unclasped his chain and flung it far
Into the keeping of the Narrow Sea,
Off Brest, across the Channel.

And smiling as it flashed and sank from sight,
'None else,' he cried, 'shall wear and mocking, say,
'This was his badge, token of England's might',
High Admiral of England.

So passed to rest. Yet while the great ships steer
Outward or home in safety as ye go,
Is it the night wind only that ye hear,
Off Brest, across the Channel?

Then be the daily task, or great or small,
What time the old shrill note awakes the decks,
So each receives the message in its call,
High Admiral of England.

'Such as pass on the seas' shall never cease,
In lawful cause secure, to come and go,
And in their passing he shall rest in peace,
Off Brest, across the Channel.

There are other recorded instances of the whistle having been used as a badge of rank up to the year 1562 when it was still worn by the Lord High Admiral. From thenceforward, however, it reverted to its original use, and was employed only as a method of passing orders. It is said that at one time the Lord High Admiral had two of these instruments, one of gold called the 'Whistle of Honour', and the other of silver, known as the 'Whistle of Command'. Falconer in his *Marine Dictionary* of 1789 describes it as 'a sort of whistle or pipe of silver or brass used by the Boatswain and his Mates to summon the sailors to their duty and direct them in the different exercises as hoisting, heaving, lowering, veering, belaying, letting go, etc.'

This peculiarly English naval instrument, badge of office or what you will, has since been adopted by almost every navy, including the Russian. The Chevalier Prégent de Bidoux was himself presented with a whistle of honour by the Queen Mother of France to commemorate his victory over Howard. Back in the days of Drake and the Armada, when the Spanish were our traditional enemies, they also followed our lead in including the whistle as part of the regalia of their admirals and captains general in charge of fleets.

In 1966 an American diving team recovered a number of objects of considerable value from the wrecks of ten Spanish treasure ships which foundered off the coast of Florida in a hurricane in 1715. One of the most interesting and valuable finds was a gold whistle attached to a slender gold chain eleven feet long, which had undoubtedly been worn by the commander of the ill-fated treasure fleet.

Since the whistle is a purely nautical instrument, it is fitting that its component parts should bear suitably nautical names, said in fact to have been conferred by Henry VIII. Thus it comprises the mouthpiece, a slender curved tube of white metal known as the 'gun', which terminates in a small barrel-shaped chamber called the 'buoy', at the top of which there is a small orifice. Attached to the lower part of the 'gun' is a thin piece of metal known as the 'keel', to which is fastened a small ring, or 'shackle'. A chain can be secured to the 'shackle', thus enabling the 'Call' to be worn round the neck.

A great variety of different notes can be obtained on a boatswain's call, and four methods are used to produce the desired

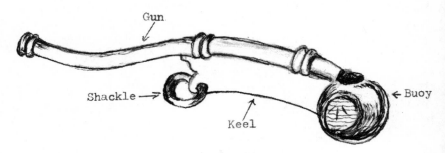

The Boatswain's Call.

effects. Blowing into the instrument with the buoy unobstructed gives the normal note. Stifling the exit of air from the orifice in the buoy with the fingers produces a throttled note. Doing the same thing, but blowing in jerks gives a warbling note like a canary, and blowing in the same fashion and vibrating the tongue produces a trilling note.

At one time there were no less than 22 calls, all with different meanings, laid down for use in the Royal Navy. These ranged from the 'Still' – which calls the hands to attention as a mark of respect or for any other purpose, and also to stop all work in order to prevent an accident – to 'Heave round the capstan', 'Mastheadmen aloft', and 'Hands to dinner'. Today these are limited to eight. The call known as 'Pipe down' sounded last thing at night as a signal for all hands to turn in, is distinct from the long single blast which is the 'Still', or the 'Hoist away' when hauling boats up to the davits by hand. A French naval manual of 1833 listed as many as 118 different orders given by the boatswain's call.

To 'pipe' really refers to the act of singing out the order required in conjunction with the use of the Call, but today the entire procedure is generally known as 'piping'. The term 'piping hot' as applied to freshly cooked food served straight from the oven owes its origin to the traditional nautical custom, still carried on in these days of shipboard dining halls and cafeteria-style messing, of piping the men to meals. Incidentally, whistling in ships is discouraged for the obvious reason that it might lead to confusion.

From salutes with the Boatswain's Call to gun salutes.

The latter are not the perquisite solely of officers of high rank in the Navy. The most senior and junior individual afloat may enjoy the doubtful honour of a one-gun salute, and this is fired when some poor wight is about to be tried by court martial on shipboard. It is known appropriately as the 'Rogue's Gun'. At the same time the Union Flag is hoisted at the yardarm to denote that the court is sitting.

In the bad old days, if the accused was found guilty of some heinous crime and sentenced to be keel-hauled – which meant being dragged bodily under the ship from one side to the other in chains – he had yet another gun salute to come. This was when he emerged from the sea when a gun was fired over his head 'as well to astonish him the more with the thunder thereof, which proveth much more offensive to him, as to give warning to all others to look out and beware'. Comparatively few victims could have managed to arrive back on the surface other than in a state of insensibility! It was also customary to fire this gun in order to muster all hands on deck in other ships present to witness a yardarm execution. A yellow flag was hoisted and kept flying until the sentence had been carried out.

Except for the 'Rogue's Gun', which of course is not a salute at all, gun salutes fired in celebration are always odd-numbered, as this was considered lucky; those fired to mark a death or funeral are even-numbered. Back in Nelson's time naval regulations required that the 'anniversary days of the Birth, Accession and Coronation of the King; of the Birth of the Queen; of the Restoration of Charles II; and *of the Gunpowder Treason* [my italics] shall be solemnised by such of HM ships as are in port with such a number of guns as the Commanding Officer present shall direct, not exceeding twenty-one.' A few years later the wording of this regulation was altered to 'the Discovery of the Gunpowder Treason', but by 1844 both this and the reference to the restoration of Charles II had disappeared. Guy Fawkes and his fellow conspirators would have been delighted to think that their abortive attempt to blow up Parliament would subsequently be honoured by the Royal Navy for the next couple of hundred years with a gun salute!

Navy regulations still specify that a flag officer or commodore in command of a squadron of warships at anchor in any port or roadstead at home or abroad may fire a morning and evening gun. If more than one flag officer or commodore is present, only the senior can fire the guns, but the others may in succession fire 'a

'The Admiral has made it Sunset, sir.' The signal to fire the Evening Gun.

volley of musketry'. In the past, immediately after the morning gun had been fired the 'Reveille' would be sounded. This custom, as far as the evening gun is concerned, originated in olden times to ensure that guns and muskets (the flint lock variety) should be properly loaded and primed before nightfall.

On one occasion during the reign of Queen Victoria this, then hallowed, naval custom almost brought about a constitutional crisis.

In August 1872 the Prince of Wales, later King Edward VII, was on board the royal yacht *Victoria & Albert* at Portland preparatory to reviewing the Channel Fleet next day. Also with him on board the royal yacht was the First Sea Lord, Admiral Sir Sydney Dacres. The First Lord himself, then Mr George Goschen, was present in the Admiralty yacht *Enchantress*. The Channel Fleet was commanded by Rear-Admiral Geoffrey Hornby flying his flag in HMS *Minotaur*.

Just as the clocks were coming up to nine p.m., when the flagship was about to fire the evening gun, it was suddenly fired instead from the royal yacht. Dacres and Hornby were furious, and the former immediately reprimanded the captain of the royal yacht in writing, and informed him that the morning gun would be fired by the *Minotaur*. A copy of this letter was sent over to Mr Goschen.

The Prince of Wales now intervened and informed the harassed First Lord that he had instructed the captain of the royal yacht, who happened to be His Serene Highness Prince Leiningen, son of a half-brother of the Queen, to fire the morning gun regardless of the consequences. It was in fact fired by the flagship and the royal yacht together.

The matter was subsequently referred by the First Lord to the Queen herself, and Mr Gladstone's Cabinet was brought in. A suggestion by the Lord Privy Seal that the Sovereign should relinquish her right of precedence at sea was countered by the Queen's acid enquiry as to whether he meant that she should be placed under the orders of her own admirals. She finally insisted that no matter how many guns were fired, or who fired them, the royal yacht must always fire first. Accordingly the Admiralty issued the face-saving order that whenever the royal yacht, or other of Her Majesty's ships wearing the Royal Standard, was present with the Fleet, 'the regulations which govern the firing of the Morning and Evening gun are to be adhered to – the time being taken from the gun which will be fired from the royal yacht'.

As far as ships' companies were concerned, whenever the evening gun was fired some messdeck wag would be sure to remark, following the sound of its report, 'It's all right, lads, the Old Man's just fallen down the main hatch!'

Warships do not dip their ensigns to each other as a form of salute, but junior ships pay their respects to their seniors by means of bands – when available – bugles, or the boatswain's call.

When steaming past a flagship or senior officer's vessel which is also under way, the junior ship makes her obeisance by sounding the 'Alert' on a bugle, or the 'Still' on a boatswain's call. The captain of the junior ship faces towards the senior vessel and salutes, all hands on her upper deck standing to attention and facing in the same direction. The ship receiving the salute replies in similar fashion, but is the first to sound the 'Carry on'.

When passing a flagship at anchor, both vessels when possible mount a Royal Marine guard and band and do the thing in style. As they draw abreast the junior ship sounds the 'Alert' and her marine guard presents arms, while the band prepares to play the ceremonial piece of music to which the admiral is entitled according to his grade and appointment. (These snatches of music, incidentally, are carefully laid down by regulation. Thus a full admiral or other flag officer appointed as a commander-in-chief is entitled to 'Rule Britannia'. A vice-admiral, rear-admiral and commodore flying a broad pennant may enjoy a portion of *Iolanthe*. These musical tributes are also played when the entitled person is paying an official visit to a warship.) By this time the 'Alert' has been sounded in the flagship, usually by its most 'tiddly' bugler just to show the junior ship how it should be done, and her guard receives the salute with sloped arms.

The smallest commissioned warship flying the White Ensign, including submarines, mine countermeasures craft, survey vessels, etc., must also observe this traditional piece of nautical etiquette, even though the best that can be done may be only a shrill wail on the boatswain's call. Occasionally, however, when the crew of a small ship includes a man who can blow a bugle, and it has been possible to scrounge, or otherwise procure, one of these instruments, it is possible to startle the lordly officer of the watch on board a flagship with a brazen blast when he expects only a weary whistle. And, of course, in the case of two 'private' ships (vessels not carrying a flag officer) passing one another, seniority to determine who should salute first is governed by the relative positions in the Navy List of both captains.

In the Navy's early days saluting between warships of different nationalities caused considerably more fuss. Ships were then 'manned', which meant that all hands lined the bulwarks at close intervals right round the upper deck. This salute had a more subtle meaning, for with the crew so disposed a ship's intentions were revealed to be friendly, since her guns could obviously not be manned at the same time. In olden days, owing to the delay in receiving despatches from home, this was a matter of some importance when it was possible for two nations to have gone to war with one another without the captains of such of their warships as happened to be on the high seas at the time becoming aware of the fact.

Nowadays 'manning ship' is reserved as a form of salute on very special occasions, such as a royal review of the Fleet. Thus they continue a practice which was first ordered for such events in Stuart times, when warships were ordered to be made 'neat and predie' (pretty), and their decks, tops, masts and shrouds thoroughly manned and, as it were, 'hung with men'.

A special form of protocol is also observed when a boat bearing an indication that an admiral or other senior naval officer is on board passes a warship. If he is a senior flag officer, such as a commander-in-chief, the 'Alert' is sounded on board the vessel being passed, when all hands on the upper deck stop work, face outboard and stand to attention. Woe betide the lubberly individual who chooses such a sacred moment to shoot a bucket of 'gash' (rubbish) overboard. For his captain will indeed be reduced to wearing sackcloth and ashes as a result. In the days of the Victorian 'spit and polish' Navy, such an occurrence would certainly have led to an official reprimand for the luckless captain.

And now to the naval hand salute itself.

It may be considered by some surprising to learn that until Queen Victoria came to the throne the only form of naval personal salute was by doffing the headgear. The old-time naval rating always removed his hat when approaching or being approached by an officer, and junior officers removed theirs when addressing or being addressed by their senior. HRH Prince William, whom we have met more than once in these pages, laid down in his orders as captain of HMS *Andromeda* in 1788 that: 'Junior officers on shore meeting a senior officer are to show proper respect by taking their hats off'. And if a punctilious old veteran like Admiral the Earl of St Vincent – 'old Jarvie' – happened to be the senior officer being so greeted, even by a common sailor, he would have doffed his in return, for he was a stickler for etiquette. Queen Victoria, however, objected to seeing men in uniform standing about bare-headed.

Thus was an end put to 'bowing and scraping' afloat, 'scraper' being the nickname given by a naval officer to his cocked hat when this article of headgear formed part of his full dress. But both officers and ratings must still remove their caps when the Articles of War are read, and when a newly appointed captain reads his commission. Ratings must always remove theirs when being formally inspected by the captain or a senior officer, and when appearing as a 'defaulter'.

No one is entirely sure of the origin of the present form of hand salute. One school of thought holds that it dates from the days when an inferior always uncovered his head to a superior, the present hand movement being the first motion of preparing to remove the headdress. Another maintains that this is a survival from the days of armour, when two warriors met and raised their visors as a mutual token of trust, since by doing so they laid themselves open to attack. Keeping the hand open showed that no weapon was concealed in the fingers. Yet a third theory is that the hand salute is a link with the Oriental custom of shading the eyes in the presence of a Very Important Personage as a humble acknowledgment of the magnificence of the Exalted One.

For the origin of this custom, then, 'you pays your money and takes your choice'.

Officers and men must also salute whenever they set foot on a warship's quarterdeck, and also when they cross the gangway on boarding. Although the former is one of the customs most strictly observed in the Royal Navy, its origin is likewise obscure and its significance has long been disputed. Some say that the salute originated in an obeisance to a crucifix situated aft in the ship. There are early pictorial records and writings which tend to uphold this theory, but it is doubtful if this custom would have survived the many religious controversies and upheavals which beset this country at different times.

It is highly improbable that a shrine or crucifix existed in any English ship from the reign of the first Queen Elizabeth, and in such circumstances the custom would have died out. Furthermore, the activities of the press-gangs alone brought together on board ship men of different religious denominations, such as Jews, Quakers, Baptists, etc. It is more probable that the quarterdeck, being the seat of authority and the position nearest to the place where the colours are displayed, the salute is paid to the Sovereign from whom that authority was received. A writer in 1842, referring to the instructions given to a newly entered midshipman, adds that: 'On coming to the quarterdeck by day or night, whether from inboard or out, the hat must be touched or lifted in compliment to the "Flag" or "Pennant" and "King's Parade" '.

The salute with the left hand was abolished in 1923, except for boatswain's mates when piping, 'so as to bring our customs in line with our wartime allies, and also to conform to the vogue in the Indian Army. Both on the Continent and among Indian and

African troops a salute given with the left hand was considered a gross insult'.*

The salute with the sword is another custom of ancient origin, but here again two schools of thought tend to collide on a matter of detail. Some hold that the salute dates back to the Crusades, and that the position of the 'Recover' is symbolical of the act of religious homage wherein the cross hilt of the sword was kissed as representing the crucifix; that holding the sword at arm's length relates to the hailing or acknowledging of the leader; and that sinking the point to the ground betokens an act of submission to superior authority. The second school of thought differs only as to the meaning of the 'Recover' which, they say, derives from the gesture of shading the eyes from the magnificence of the superior being.

* *A Few Naval Customs, Expressions, Traditions & Superstitions*, Beckett.

CHAPTER XII

The Black Book

Some years ago a book was published which purported to give the true origins of a host of naval terms and expressions. In it the author, who seems to have had his leg well and truly pulled by naughty sailors in his quest for copy, stated solemnly that the *Black Book of the Admiralty*, about which he had heard rumour, was a record kept by Their Lordships over the years of all the 'blacks' put up by sailors. To 'put up a black', meaning in modern jargon to make a boob, was an expression common in the Royal Air Force during the Second World War.

But this is where the hapless author himself put up a colossal 'black', for the *Admiralty Black Book* – and there is indeed such a volume – is the ancient muniment book containing the 'Rules for the Office of Lord High Admiral; Ordinances for the Admiralty in Time of War; the Laws of Oleron; Rules for the Office of Constable and Marshal; and other Rules and Precedents', dating from the fifteenth century, printed in French, Latin and English, and preserved in the Public Record Office.

Promulgated about the year 1160 by Eleanor of Aquitaine, wife of King Henry II of England, the Laws of Oleron, based on the decisions of the Merchant Court of the little island of Oleron, which lies in the Bay of Biscay close to the west coast of France, were accepted as maritime law in north-western Europe from the latter half of the twelfth century. Their prestige in Britain was especially high. In plain commonsense language, they codified the principles that should govern relations between the parties concerned in maritime trade: shipmasters, mariners, owners and merchants, and prescribed the action that might properly be taken in various contingencies.

Over the centuries the Laws of Oleron have gradually been superseded, although certain aspects of modern maritime law may be traced to them, including the Naval Discipline Act, codified under Charles II as the 'Articles of War'. These define offences under naval law, and govern naval court martial procedure. They are familiar to every serving sailor, since they must be read out to the ship's company of a warship at the first opportunity after commissioning, and thereafter displayed in a prominent position.

The often misquoted preamble to these stated that they had been drawn up for the government of 'the Navy whereon, under the good providence of God, the wealth, safety and strength of the kingdom chiefly depend'. In 1956 when the Naval Discipline Act was re-written to meet modern conditions of life in the Royal Navy, the words 'so much' were substituted for 'chiefly'. But this does not diminish the importance of the role of Britain's first line of defence.

The original Articles of War numbered thirty-six, for the transgression of which no less than twenty-two carried the death penalty. With the passage of time others have been added, but only very few today carry the death penalty. In the bad old days when stern and repressive measures were considered necessary, the sentence for murder, for example, required the assassin to be tied to the corpse of his victim and hove into the sea; or, if on land, to be buried alive. For drawing a knife to stab another, or actually stabbing him, the offender was to lose a hand. For striking another with his fist, the aggressor was to be ducked three times from the yardarm. For defiance of, vilifying, or swearing at his fellows, a man had to pay one ounce of silver for each offence.

For robbery and theft the convicted individual was to have boiling pitch poured over his head and a shower of feathers shaken over him, and to be cast ashore at the first point of land. For a repeated offence of sleeping on watch, 'he shall be hanged to the bowsprit end of the ship in a basket with a can of beer, a loaf of bread and a sharp knife, and choose to hang there until he starve or cut himself into the sea'. Punishments for previous offences of this nature were painful and uncomfortable – if less drastic – consisting of 'grampussing', or half drowning the man by pouring seawater into his sleeves while his arms were held above his head, or spreadeagling him in the weather rigging.

In early times disciplinary powers were vested in the commander of a fleet or squadron, who dealt with the more serious offences personally or through a 'Council of War', the origin of the present-day court martial. Powers of punishment for less serious crimes were delegated to individual captains. These powers were required to be exercised in accordance with 'the laws and customs of the sea', and according to the gravity of the offence. Malefactors could be kept in 'bilboes' (fetters) for as long as the captain wished; made to fast; ducked from the yardarm, and keel-hauled.

Flogging was of course widely used as a punishment for even the most trivial misdemeanours, the most terrible form being a flogging through the fleet. If a man survived such an ordeal, he would be unfit for further service when he was able to leave the sick bay, and usually died within a short time. Incidentally, when we talk of not being able to 'swing a cat' in a confined space, this does not refer to the animal itself, but to the cat-o'nine-tails used in the Navy to administer a flogging. And to 'let the cat out of the bag' meant removing this dread instrument from the baize bag in which it was usually kept. Men sentenced to flogging were often spreadeagled over a gun to receive this punishment. They were then said to 'Marry the Gunner's daughter'.

The number of lashes at an official flogging was left to the captain, but for theft a man might be made to 'run the gauntlet'. After receiving a dozen strokes with the 'cat', he was made to proceed between two lines of sailors each armed with a rope's end. The master-at-arms preceded him with a drawn sword pointed at his chest in order to slow up his progress, until every man had beaten him. After receiving another dozen strokes with the 'cat', he had to make a second journey down the other side of the ship. 'Running the gauntlet', from which is derived the present-day colloquialism, was officially abolished in the Navy in 1813.

There were other peculiar and unpleasant forms of punishment for the unfortunate sailor who transgressed the regulations. For example, any man convicted of telling a lie could be hoisted up to the main stay with a broom and shovel tied to his back, where he had to hang for half an hour while his shipmates cried, 'A liar! A liar!' at him. In 1672 two seamen who had stolen a piece of beef were lashed to the main mast with their hands tied behind them and a piece of raw beef hung around their necks. There they had to remain for two hours while the ship's company came up one by one and rubbed them over the mouth with the raw meat.

But of course in a mixed community of seamen forming the ships' companies of those days, suffering much hardship, it was inevitable

'Defaulters' being held on the quarterdeck of a Victorian man-of-war.

that discipline could not be universally good at all times. When the *Mary Rose*, the first of Henry VIII's 'big-gun ships', capsized at Spithead in 1545 under the appalled gaze of that monarch, the opinion of her captain, Sir Peter Carew, of her company was 'a sort of knaves' whom he could not rule. 'They soe maligned and disdayned one the other that, refusing to doe that they should doe, they were careless to doe that they oughte to doe, and so contendinge in spite, perished in frowardnesse'. More than one Elizabethan sea captain complained that his ship was manned by a 'loose rabble', and 'a vagrant, lewd and disorderly ragged regiment of common rogues'.

Today the Articles of War no longer threaten ferocious punishments for naval misdemeanours. Justice in the Navy is humane, fair and impartial, and it speaks volumes for the modern naval court martial, evolved from the harsh regimes of past centuries, that the committee which overhauled the Naval Discipline Act in the 1950s found that it enjoyed a high degree of prestige in the twentieth-century Navy.

A traditional custom still in use at the court martial of a naval officer is that of using his sword, which has to be delivered up at the outset of his trial and lie unsheathed on the table before his judges, to indicate to him their verdict. If the point is turned towards him, he has been found guilty; but if the hilt confronts him when he is brought back into the courtroom, the verdict is acquittal. This delicate hint of the shape of things to come dates from sterner times when beheading awaited a luckless offender on shore should a court decide against him in a capital trial. On leaving the place of trial he was preceded by the headsman, who carried the edge of the axe towards the prisoner if death was to be his fate, or away from him if imprisonment only was the sentence.

For a maritime nation whose everyday language is interlarded with terms and expressions which owe their origin to their seagoing ancestors, Britons are guilty of making a good many errors in nautical matters, which are even more widely disseminated through the media of press, television and broadcasting. At the same time it must be admitted that some serving sailors are themselves to blame in helping to perpetuate these inaccuracies. Those, for example, who refer to a warship without the prefix 'HMS', or that grammatical necessity, the definite article.

This particular error almost always crops up in written form, and frequently in films, plays and dramas of the sea. For no sailor makes the claim in shipboard conversation that he once served 'in *Ark Royal*', or went 'aboard *Leander*'. The absence of the appropriate prefix appears even more ludicrous when subtracted from those well known epics of prose and poetry *The Wreck of the Hesperus*, or *The Mutiny on the Bounty*.

Reference to a warship by name without prefix traditionally indicates only her captain. In olden times he *was* the ship. For, after touting for an appointment afloat from all those of his friends and patrons who possessed the necessary influence when a war appeared imminent – since in peacetime the bulk of our warships were always laid up 'in ordinary' as an economy measure – it was up to the captain to get his ship into commission and to sea by fair means or foul, or lose the job. Hence, of course, the necessity of instituting a 'hot press' in order to obtain a crew.

As already mentioned, the correct reply to the gangway hail by the coxswain of a boat conveying a warship's captain about his business in a harbour or fleet anchorage at night is simply the name of the ship he commands. When a commander-in-chief or other flag officer sends a signal to the captains of the ships of his fleet or squadron, the message is addressed to those vessels by name, e.g., *Tiger, Ark Royal, Salisbury*, and not to 'The Commanding Officers, HM Ships *Tiger, Ark Royal, Salisbury*, etc', thus saving valuable time. To emphasise this particular point still further, when the Duke of Edinburgh was serving in the Mediterranean Fleet in command of the frigate *Magpie*, he was always addressed by his senior officer in signals simply as *Magpie*. Similarly, when the Prince of Wales commanded the minehunter *Bronington*, he, too, became simply *Bronington* in signals addressed to him as commanding officer. And in operational orders and official despatches, captains become the ships they command. These are the only occasions when a ship's name properly appears without the prefix 'HMS' or the definite article.

A ghastly nautical solecism is not infrequently perpetrated by the publicity departments of shipping companies and tourist agencies. 'Come cruising,' they invite in alluring advertisements, 'on our ss *Nonsuch*'. 'On', you observe shudderingly, not 'in'. What kind of vessel, then, is the ss *Nonsuch*? If she was a submarine the passengers would have precious little chance to enjoy their cruise, since the moment the vessel submerged they would be washed off!

This particular horror once formed the subject of a wartime illustrated joke in *Punch*. Sprawled on a couple of roughly nailed-together planks in mid-ocean after their ship had obviously been torpedoed are an elderly sailor wearing a disgusted expression on his face, and a bright-looking youth clutching a writing pad and pencil. 'Do you,' he is asking his companion, 'say *in* or *on* a raft?'

Even Water Rat in *The Wind in the Willows* knew the correct form. 'Believe me, my young friend', he tells Mole, 'there is nothing – absolutely nothing – half so much worth doing as simply messing about in boats'. *In*, you notice, not *on*. In or on a ship? Why not 'on' a house? A curiously common error for a seagoing race like the British to continue to make.

Many a girl friend or fond relative has shivered a sailor's timbers by asking sweetly, 'What boat are you on?' There are, or were, as the seasoned tar is well aware, only two kinds of 'boat' in the Royal

Navy when the term is applied to seagoing ships: destroyers and submarines. Unhappily the former have now all disappeared from the Fleet. If, however, an officer or rating is attached to the Submarine Service, he belongs to 'the Trade', and the underwater craft in which he serves are always referred to as 'boats'. And those who serve in nuclear submarines are apt to refer to them as 'nukes'. Destroyers began to be dubbed 'boats' ever since the first torpedo-boat destroyer made its startling appearance towards the end of last century. Today their place has been taken by a new type of workhorse known as the frigate, which seems to have acquired no special nickname. One sure way of avoiding error in this matter of 'boats' is to remember that boats can be carried by ships, but not ships by boats.

Then there is the little matter of the 'Skipper'. Regrettably, ocean liners – those magnificent floating hotels of more gracious times – are becoming fewer and fewer, but how their captains and those mariners who command modern supertankers, for example, must growl inwardly when they see and hear themselves described in press and broadcast reports as 'Skipper'. Perhaps reporters and commentators consider that this (incorrect) title sounds so much more nautical.

There is in fact only one real Skipper, and he is the man who commands a trawler or drifter whose business is wresting fish from the sea, for he holds an official certificate of competency as such. The Master of the *Queen Elizabeth II*, or of some half-million-ton tanker or cumbersome container ship, is no more qualified to command a fishing vessel than a trawler skipper is to take charge of an ocean liner – unless the latter has also qualified for his Master's certificate, and the former for his fishing 'ticket'.

The commander of a Merchant Navy vessel may be given the courtesy title of 'Captain', unless he already holds that substantive rank in the Royal Naval Reserve, in which case his ship will be permitted to fly the Blue Ensign instead of the 'Red Duster'. But in the eyes of the law he is always the 'Master under God', as his ship's articles continue quaintly to phrase his title. And if he happens to be the senior master of his particular shipping line, his full title is 'Commodore Master', and not just 'Commodore'.

As for the Navy, the commanding officer is frequently referred to unofficially as 'the Skipper' or 'the Bloke' by the men of the lower deck; occasionally as the 'Old Man', however young in years he may be; and customarily by the wardroom as 'the Owner'; and his cabin is still traditionally referred to as 'the Cuddy'. He may even be called 'Father', although strictly this nickname should be applied only to an admiral. The commander of a large warship, such as an aircraft carrier or of a naval shore establishment, as opposed to the captain, is known as 'the Bloke'; while the First Lieutenant is always 'Jimmy the One', and sometimes the 'Chief Housemaid'.

There used to be many other nicknames for the various officers of a warship, but with the passage of time and the abolition of certain ranks, these have largely died out. But at any Royal Naval Association gathering, however, all old-timers will instantly recognise them.

'Guns', or 'Gunnery Jack', was the nickname of the ship's gunnery officer, and 'Torps' the torpedo officer. 'Ping' was the anti-submarine specialist, a more modern term originating from the sound of the *asdic*, or *sonar*. The chaplain was the 'Sky Pilot', or 'Sin Bosun'; while the boatswain himself, today a rank only to be found on the Retired List, was 'Tommy Pipes', and his contemporary, the gunner, 'Old Blue Lights'. When the rank of warrant cookery officer was instituted, he was at once dubbed the 'Custard Bosun'; but he, too, no longer exists in the modern Navy.

The senior engineer officer of a ship was always 'the Chief', and his second in command 'the Senior'. Junior engineer officers were the 'Plumbers'. The senior Royal Marine Officer was known as 'the Major', and he might well have held that rank in a capital ship. In Nelsonic times he was called 'Cheeks' because of the rather revealing uniform coat he wore.

A lieutenant of the executive branch not qualified as a specialist was known as a 'Salt Horse', while a lieutenant-commander similarly unspecialised would be dubbed a 'Spunyarn Major'. A dental officer rejoiced in the obvious nickname of 'Toothy'; an instructor officer as 'Schoolie', and the navigating officer as 'the Pilot' or 'Navvie'. The ship's bugler or Royal Marine drummer was always known as 'Sticks'; the chief boatswain's mate as 'the Buffer'; the Master-at-Arms as 'the Jaunty', from the French *gendarme* or 'John Damme'; and his minions, the regulating staff, originally ships' corporals, as 'Crushers' – a discourteous reference to the alleged size of their feet.

A signal rating was invariably 'Bunts', from the material of which his flags were made, and sometimes as the 'Bunting-Tosser'. A leading rate is a 'Killick', said to be the name for a small anchor, since this is his distinguishing rank badge; a Royal Marine is a 'Bootneck', 'Turkey' or 'Leatherneck', for reasons explained in a later chapter; while a soldier is described either as a 'Grabby', 'Swaddy' or 'Pongo'. During the Second World War he also became known afloat as a 'Brown Job'. But he could have his own back on the 'matlows' in the matter of nicknames by dubbing them 'Sand-scratchers' from the practice once common of scrubbing the decks with sand; or 'Webfoot'. There were of course a good many other nicknames which date back over the years but are no longer used, and fresh ones which became current during World War II but have sunk into disuse.

Story writers who from time to time wish to introduce a sailor into their yarns have a habit of dubbing these heroes 'Nobby' Clark, 'Pincher' Martin, or perhaps 'Dusty' Miller. But their acquaintance with nautical sounding nicknames usually ends there. Yet there are in fact a host of such artificial 'tallies' in the naval service. ('Tally' from cap tally, or cap ribbon.)

Whether the practice of conferring such nicknames can be said to be purely naval in origin is open to question, but since the 'Andrew' is the oldest of the armed forces, and since in the days of the press-gangs almost every other able-bodied male in Britain served afloat at some time or other during his lifetime, it may well be.

'Nobby' for attachment to the surname Clark can also be hooked on to anyone born with the surname Ewart or Hewitt. In fact this particular tally can probably be claimed as pure Navy, since it dates from a famous old naval captain whose name was Charles Edward Ewart. This gentleman was such a stickler for spit and polish in the ships he commanded that the appellation was a natural.

In those days captains of warships frequently took their own private flock of poultry to sea with them for later eating. These were kept, along with other livestock which might be embarked, in the 'manger', a compartment at the forward end of the lower gun deck. On one occasion 'Nobby' Ewart let fly at his unfortunate coxswain for not grooming his fowls and falling them in on deck for Sunday

Divisions along with the rest of the ship's company. How to line up a platoon of lively poultry and keep them properly dressed by the right might have floored a lesser man than 'Nobby's' coxswain. But on the following Sunday this resourceful individual fell in his birds on a plank, duly smartened up in their best plumage, and kept in position by means of a staple fastened over the toes of the chickens, and tintacks through the webs of the ducks!

Other traditional nominal labels attached by sailors to their shipmates' surnames are 'Bandy' Evans; 'Slinger' Woods; 'Knocker' White; 'Dodger' Long from dodge a-long; 'Spike' Sullivan; 'Wiggy' Bennett; 'Cosher' Hinds; 'Buck' Taylor; 'Sharkey' Ward; 'Jumper' Collins; 'Shiner' Wright; 'Daisy' Bell; 'Spud' Murphy; 'Chats' Harris; 'Jimmy' Green; 'Kitty' Wells; 'Rusty' Steel; and 'Tug' Wilson. 'Tosh' was once commonly attached to anyone named Gilbert. But this was not always regarded as a complimentary nickname, since 'toshing' was an old-time term for the practice of stealing the copper from the bottoms of sheathed ships.

The origins of some of these naval nicknames are obvious. Thus 'Brigham' Young, after the founder of the Mormons; 'General' Booth, of the Salvation Army; 'Sweeney' Todd, of 'Demon Barber' fame; 'Pedlar' Palmer, once a well known boxer; and 'Bill' Bailey, 'Nellie' Dean and 'Dolly' Gray, after certain one-time popular songs. There were also 'Bogy' Knight; 'Taff' Evans; 'Dicky' Bird; 'Topsy' Turner; 'Bob' Tanner; 'Darby' Kelly; 'Happy' Day; 'Froggy' French; 'Pony' Moore; 'Bungy' Williams; 'Pasha' Baker, and 'Nancy' Lee. Anyone tall is dubbed 'Lofty', and anyone short, 'Tich'. A sailor with a large head is usually known, behind his back at least, as 'Nutty'; any Scot as 'Jock'; Welshman 'Taffy'; Irishman as 'Paddy'; a native of Newcastle as 'Geordie', and anyone with a strong West Country accent as 'Jagger'.

CHAPTER XIII

'Bottles', Beards and Fun and Games

Most of us at one time or another during our careers have found ourselves being 'torn off a strip', or at the receiving end of a 'blast' from someone in authority for doing something stupid or wrong. In the Navy this kind of verbal dressing-down is known as a 'bottle'. It is also a bit of rather old Navy. For, years ago when the 'wooden wall' sailor got himself into a minor scrape on shipboard he found himself being issued by Authority with 'a dose from the foretopman's bottle', to give the phrase in full. Just what the legendary foretopman is supposed to have kept in the said bottle we are not told. But obviously it must have been a very caustic fluid.

In those days the foretopmen in a ship were individuals with personalities, and on a par with the upper yardmen, the most skilled seamen who were normally detailed to man the upper yards. 'The beau ideal of a thoroughbred man-o'war's man ... whose element is so peculiarly the sea ... distinguishable from ordinary tars by a tie (queue) reaching down to his loins of the diameter of a medium-sized handspike before the fashion of queues was on the wane'.* With the disappearance of the pigtail, these 'taut hands' also popularised a special hair style for sailors. Known as the 'foretopman's lock', this was a quiff of oiled hair carefully curled and worn flat on the forehead. But the male fashion of brushing the hair straight back, so that an individual sporting this style, commented the old-timers sourly, resembled 'a rat that has eaten his way through a keg of butter', banished the 'foretopman's lock' for ever.

During the Second World War the practice of growing a beard became all the rage in the Navy; even the Duke of Edinburgh wore one when he was serving in the Far East. After all, even the most chairborne warrior might hope to be mistaken for a tough, seagoing submariner if he could manage to cultivate a handsome growth of

* *Service Afloat*, Anon.

whiskers. Incidentally, the nickname of any bearded individual in a ship was generally 'Skers' (the after-part of the word 'whiskers'), and his facial growth was referred to as a 'set'.

But although beards have long been associated with sailors – and the individual whose hirsute countenance first made famous in 1891 the package design of a well known brand of cigarettes has greatly contributed to the tradition – they are in fact only just over a century old as an approved naval facial adornment.

The Crimean War, during which many hundreds of sailors served ashore in naval brigades with the Army, did much to popularise this *military* fashion afloat, but it was still unofficial. There were, however, says Commander W.E. May, RN, 'a lot of isolated instances of facial adornment in the Navy before that'.* Captain Cook refers to beards in his ships; our old friend Captain William Walpole, the eccentric commanding officer of HMS *Vernon*, forbade shaving in his ship during a period of detachment from the Fleet in the Mediterranean. In 1827 the officers of a sloop serving in the West Indies sported moustaches, as also in 1856 did one admiral. But the Admiralty remained adamant that sailors' faces should be clean-shaven.

It is related that when gunnery specialist Captain William Moorsom, RN, inventor of the percussion shell, returned from service in the Black Sea sporting a luxurious beard, he called as was customary on the First Sea Lord at the Admiralty. The Great Man, then Admiral Sir Maurice Fitzhardinge Berkeley, looked up from his desk one morning to find Moorsom peering enquiringly at him from behind his whiskers. The First Sea Lord slowly paled with rage and astonishment. Then he waved the intruder away with the curt remark, 'Horse Guards, next door!'

It was Queen Victoria who brought about the change officially. The captain of the royal yacht, then His Serene Highness the Prince of Leiningen, son of the Queen's half-brother, whom we have already met, had informed her that 'more bad language is made use of during the quarter of an hour devoted to shaving than during any other part of the day', and outlined the difficulties of the sailor trying to scrape his weather-beaten cheeks with an inferior razor on a rolling deck with only a small piece of looking glass to peer into.

* *R.N. Hirsute History*, Mariner's Mirror, August 1975.

The Queen put the matter to the First Lord of the Admiralty, the Right Honourable Hugh Childers, who in turn consulted the Admiralty Board, who referred it to the naval commanders-in-chief. All but two of the latter objected to the wearing of beards. Nevertheless, the First Lord, who knew his Queen, went ahead and drafted an order which he submitted to Her Majesty for approval. 'The Queen thanks Mr Childers very much for his communication on the subject of beards,' she wrote on 17th June 1869. 'She thinks the order will do extremely well. Her own personal feeling would be for beards without moustaches, as the latter have rather a soldier-like appearance; but then the object in view would not be obtained, viz., to prevent the necessity for shaving. Therefore it had best be as proposed, the entire beard, only it should be kept short and clean'. But one important amendment was to be included. 'The Queen wishes to make one additional observation respecting the beards, viz., that on no account should moustaches be allowed without beards. That must be clearly understood'.

And so, on 24th June 1869, the Admiralty reluctantly issued the following order to the Fleet:

BEARDS AND MOUSTACHES IN THE ROYAL NAVY

The Lords Commissioners of the Admiralty have had under their consideration the provisions of Chapter 44, Article 43, page 336 of the Regulations, forbidding the wearing of Beards and Moustaches by Officers and Men of the Fleet.

Representations having been made to their Lordships that it would conduce to the health and comfort of men, under many circumstances of service, were they to be permitted to discontinue the use of the Razor on board her Majesty's Ships, they have been pleased to issue the following Regulations:

1. Clause 43, Chapter 44 of the Regulations is repealed, and Officers and Men on board her Majesty's Ships, including the Royal Marines when embarked, will in future be permitted to wear Beards and Moustaches.

2. In all cases, when the permission granted in Clause 1 is taken advantage of, the use of the Razor must be entirely discontinued. Moustaches are not to be worn without the Beard, nor is the Beard to be worn without the Moustaches.

3. The hair of Beard, Moustaches and Whiskers, is to be kept

British sailor of the Crimean War period sporting a beard.

Royal Fleet Reserve man of World War I wearing
his civilian moustache.

well cut and trimmed, and not too long for cleanliness. The
Captain is to give such directions as seem to him desirable upon
these heads, and to establish, so far as may be practicable,
uniformity as to length of the Hair, Beards, Moustaches and
Whiskers of his Men; observing that those Men who do not avail
themselves of the permission to wear Beard and Moustaches will
wear their Hair and Whiskers as heretofore.

4. Officers of Divisions will take special care that the provisions
of Clauses 2 and 3 are strictly attended to by such of their Men
as may avail themselves of the permission contained in Clause 1,
and failure in those respects is to be considered an offence under
Article C in the Table of Summary Punishments.

5. Royal Marines on shore will follow the Regulations of the
Army with regard to Beard and Moustaches.

6. Their Lordships desire that it may be distinctly understood
that the permission now given to wear Beards and Moustaches *is
not necessarily to be considered as permanent* (my italics), and that if
neatness and cleanliness are not observed this order will be
revoked.

And so it remains in this hirsute age despite the occasional rebellious rumble from the more junior of present-day Navy men. .

In general, sailors' hair styles have varied with the changes of fashion on shore. During Cromwell's Commonwealth most wore their hair cropped just as did the 'Roundheads'. The nautical Beau Brummell would probably have earned himself more than a mere 'bottle' if he had dared to step out of line anyway. But with the restoration of Charles II, sailors once again followed the example of their officers. In imitation of the King and his Court the latter took to wearing full and flowing wigs. The sailors contented themselves with growing their hair long.

Then, around the middle of the eighteenth century, naval officers began to wear the fashionable queue, and the men followed suit. The more 'tiddly' ratings used an eelskin as a heart when making up their pigtails, and some even wove in rope yarns to increase the size and length. This fashion called for a good deal of trouble to be taken with one's appearance, and close friends would tie each other's pigtails for special occasions. From this practice they began to be dubbed 'Tiemates'. Later when the pigtail ceased to be worn, the term 'Raggies' to describe particular chums took its place. The new word derived from the more mundane practice of two friends sharing their brightwork cleaning rags. If they quarrelled, they were said to have 'parted brass rags'.

In the past certain senior naval officers with the reputations of being 'characters' have occasionally overstepped the mark in inflicting their idiosyncrasies upon the officers and men under their command – but they haven't always got away with it. In the early 1920s Rear-Admiral David Norris, known to all because of his small stature and fiery temperament, as 'Cock', was appointed to a battle squadron in the Mediterranean Fleet. He had commanded a small flotilla of warships operating against the Bolsheviks in the Caspian Sea in 1918-19, during which he sustained a wound which resulted in a permanent shortening of his right arm. Whenever he went ashore, a small dinghy was towed behind his barge so that he could row himself back to the ship as a form of therapy.

'Cock' Norris was therefore a 'Character', one of his idiosyncrasies being an obsession about sailors' hair styles, even considering the then conservative 'short back and sides' far too long. During his stay on board another battleship of the squadron while his flagship was in dock, he insisted on accompanying the captain on his inspection of the ship's company divisions on Sundays, when they had to take their caps off. Invariably he had a complaint to make about the length of their hair.

When his flagship was finally ready to receive him, and he was about to quit the vessel which had temporarily flown his flag, he informed her captain – to the latter's disgust – that he would be officially inspecting her within the next few days. 'As you love me,' were his parting words to his erstwhile flag captain, 'get their hair cut!'

Warning was duly passed on to the ship's company, and the ship's torpedo division privately determined to take Norris literally at his word. Just before the inspection, which was to include a 'muster by the open list' (see Chapter 2), which would bring all hands individually under the admiral's piercing gaze, all had their heads shaved in Yul Brunner style – a fashion they dubbed 'the Norris bingle'.

On the appointed day of the inspection, some thirty to forty sailors with bald, shiny craniums solemnly marched in succession past their admiral. The latter's complexion gradually turned red, then blue, then purple as his veins visibly swelled, while the captain and officers, who had had no prior warning of what to expect, experienced the greatest difficulty in keeping straight faces. The admiral made no comment then or later, but it was noticeable thereafter that 'Cock' Norris lost all further interest in the length of a sailor's hair!

Oddly enough perhaps, sailors are often intensely proud of their 'Characters'. If such a one should be a captain, his ship's company will 'howl' (complain) continuously among themselves about his eccentricities. Yet should anyone else in the squadron or fleet dare to utter a derogatory word about him, they will go into action in his defence with the utmost ferocity. Similar emotions are apt to be aroused about various flag officers. This is why, all these years after World War I, there are still a 'Jellicoe faction' and equally fervid 'Beatty men' who will spring to the defence of their respective heroes at the drop of a hat.

'Tell me', one flag officer, with a passion for evolutions who had recently taken over command of a cruiser squadron and subjected its ships to a week of unremitting night and day drills and exercises, demanded of his coxswain, 'what do they think of me? Come along, man', he barked impatiently as the chief petty officer strove to frame his reply as diplomatically as he could.

'Well, sir,' he replied at last – after all, he could only be disrated – 'they say you're a bloody old bastard!'

'Old?' exclaimed the admiral in a pained voice, 'dammit, I'm only fifty-one'.

Throughout the centuries, despite the hardships they were called upon to endure, British sailors have always been 'men of gay and joyous temperament ... prone to sentiment and romance, and of a nature inclined to quaint unconventionality'. In the days of the Elizabethan sea-dogs, dicing, card-playing and every kind of gambling was prohibited on shipboard, so something else was needed. Musicians were carried and seamen encouraged to sing and dance. As recently as 1906 the Admiralty published an official naval song book, which included more than seventy titles, among them 'Life on the Ocean Wave', 'Lass that Loves a Sailor', 'Tom Bowling', 'Widdicombe Fair', 'Home, Sweet Home' and 'John Peel'. It cost sixpence a copy, but there was a smaller edition at fourpence. Old-time sailors also staged plays of their own, forerunners of the modern ship's concert.

It was in those early days that the hornpipe originated. Reference to it as a folk dance can be found in the works of Chaucer, and its association with the sea began in the fifteenth century. The small space required for the dance and the fact that no partners are necessary made it particularly suitable for shipboard use. The hornpipe was danced in Drake's day, and Captain Cook on his voyages of exploration encouraged his men to dance the hornpipe as a form of health-giving exercise in the cramped space of his tiny ships.

Among the earliest of English ballets was *The Jig of the Ship* 'which appears to have been a characteristic dance performed by sailors at the conclusion of a play', from which the hornpipe probably originated. Pepys saw the ballet at the Duke of York's Theatre and learnt the tune. The steps of the dance were adapted to demonstrate the seaman's duties: coiling, climbing and hauling ropes; running up the ratlines; clearing up decks; rowing a boat;

keeping lookout, etc. King George V, the Queen's grandfather, received instruction in hornpipe dancing as part of his training as a naval cadet on board HMS *Britannia*. While rarely danced at sea nowadays, it has not entirely died out in the push-button Navy of the seventies.

There are probably few people today, except the most elderly of retired naval officers and pensioner ratings who can remember a certain shipboard game, which was equally popular with officers on guest nights and the lower deck in off-duty hours. No record of it is to be found in that *vade-mecum* of nautical gamesmanship *Sports and Recreations in the Royal Navy*. The game was called 'Priest of the Parish', and no one knows how it began. Possibly it had been learnt from French prisoners during the Napoleonic wars; more than 18,000 of these had been confined in hulks and elsewhere in the Portsmouth district alone between 1793 and 1815.

The game required no props, other than an instrument for awarding punishment, an intimate knowledge of the ritual, and a certain degree of mental concentration. The players, of whom there could be almost any number, squatted on the deck in a circle, the chief member being the 'Priest' himself, armed with a 'stonachy' – usually a knotted napkin, or, if a Lower Deck 'Parish', a rope's end. Next to him sat a specially favoured individual known as 'Man John', whose function was temporarily to assume the Priest's duties should he be human enough to err in the conduct of his Parish.

The game commenced with the Priest striking the deck with his 'stonachy' and declaring the Parish open. He then pointed to every member of the circle in turn, inviting each to announce his 'Cap'. Thus there would be Messrs 'Red Cap', 'Blue Cap', 'White Cap', 'Green Cap', 'Black Cap', 'University Cap', 'Knee Cap', 'Percussion Cap', 'Night Cap', and so on. The nominal roll having thus been called, the Priest then struck the deck again and declaimed: 'The Priest of the Parish has lost his considering cap. Who claims this very fine piece of money? Some say this and some say that, but I say – Mister Blue Cap!'

The individual thus unexpectedly addressed was required instantly to salute and riposte: 'Who, me, sir?'

Priest: 'Yes, you, sir.'

Blue Cap: 'You lie, sir.'

Priest: 'Who then, sir?'

Blue Cap: (hoping to catch his *vis-à-vis* napping) 'Mr Red Cap!'

The dialogue then switched to the latter, each 'Cap' watching closely in the hope of catching him out in some deviation from the set ritual. If one succeeded, he yelled: 'Watch Red Cap!'

The Priest now halted the proceedings with a blow on the deck with his 'stonachy' and announced: 'Mr Red Cap watched by (say) Mr White Cap. Who claims this very fine piece of money?'

The sycophant then declaimed unctuously: 'I, White Cap, claim that very fine piece of money. Likewise Mr Red Cap who, bringing a very fine flipper to the front did during the course of this most divine ceremony make a complete and utter ballsup of his dialogue in that he did (here followed details of the offence). I therefore beg leave to award him one good flip over the behind.'

If the punishment was approved, the Priest handed over the 'stonachy' to White Cap. Red Cap was required to rise and bend over to receive a hefty swipe from his tormentor. The 'stonachy' was then returned to the Priest with a salute and the words: 'All just dues and debts duly paid, most noble lord.'

Since the game had to be played as fast as possible, even experienced players were often caught out in some error of ritual. To liven things up, players could be 'watched' for other offences, such as saluting another player instead of the Priest, squatting with crossed legs, smoking while addressing the 'Parish', or even being out of the rig of the day.

There was no doubt as to the popularity of the game, and its echoes are apt to linger on in the present-day Navy – if unwittingly – for a boastful individual is still sometimes referred to as 'a good flip to the front', and an article recovered after being mislaid as 'a very fine piece of money'.

But in the 1920s the game was on the way out, and, for the lower deck at least, a successor on the way in. In the dog watches one day on board their ship four sailors sat down at their mess table and began to play a game with a board, dice and counters. Onlookers gathered round to watch as the language became heated, tension rose, and excitement grew. Ludo had come afloat.

Normally this innocuous parlour game requires each of four players to propel a number of coloured counters, one at a time, round a set course on the board from 'Home' to 'Base', moving them along so many spaces at a time as dictated by a throw of the dice. But the rules also direct that if a counter belonging to one of the players alights on a space already occupied by one of the counters of an opponent, the counter *in situ* shall ignominiously return 'Home', there to await the throwing of a double-six by its owner before being able to make a fresh start.

Since sailors welcome opposition, the nautical exponents of the game began to concentrate more on 'hucking' their opponents' counters off the board rather than peacefully navigating the course to 'Base', and the lower deck name for this indoor sport was ready-made: 'Huckers'. ('Hucking' is in fact a dyed-in-the-wool Navy term, and in the days of wooden men-of-war to 'huck', or hog, the vessel was to scrub the barnacles and other marine growths off her bottom with stiff brushes made of birch twigs while she was in graving dock, or being careened in an anchorage.) Then some wit dreamed up the idea of playing the game on a giant scale, and 'Grand Uckers' (the aitch having been dropped) was born.

When the third *Ark Royal*, so frequently 'sunk' by Nazi propaganda in World War II, was launched in 1937, she carried in

The third *Ark Royal*. Sunk by U-boat 14 November 1941.

'Grand 'Uckers' at Wembley, 1954. A boatswain's mate moves a living 'counter' with the air of his rope's end.

her recreation space official Admiralty recognition of the Navy's post popular off-watch diversion. For part of the deck covering of this compartment was designed in the form of a giant Ludo board. Dressed in grotesque rigs, and attended by 'seconds' to groom them for the physical effort required to shake and throw cubic foot-sized dice in a mess tub, players now began to represent ships, and even squadrons, in Uckers matches.

In 1954 the Navy staged its largest and most colourful version of the game at Wembley before an enthusiastic crowd of sightseers. No fewer than 64 players participated, backed up by half a dozen buglers, two volunteer brass bands, and the band of the Coldstream Guards. The 'board' on that occasion measured no less than 3,600 square feet in area and weighed just over a ton. The dice, which had to be shaken in a 5ft bin, weighed 16½lbs and required the efforts of two men to throw. The 'uckers', or counters, were represented by live sailors in fancy rigs, who were kept in order on their way round the board by boatswain's mates wearing the dress of Nelson's day and wielding rope's ends. The umpire, known for some esoteric reason, as Lili Marlene, was mounted on a full-sized model elephant, which could move not only its head, ears and legs, but also pump foam from its trunk. Motive power was provided by four engineer mechanics, whose movements were directed by means of engine-room telegraph bells.

Since gunrooms have now vanished from the Fleet, senior officers are no longer required to risk a slipped disc, if nothing worse, by climbing through a chair after taking dinner with the 'young gentlemen' on guest nights. Wardroom guest night fun and games are usually restricted these days to 'cock-fighting', 'dry land rowing', and, in shore establishments, inscribing one's name on the ceiling with the aid of a pyramid of mess furniture. Concert parties of course continue to live on, fuelled with ideas largely taken from popular television series which have been given a suitably nautical flavour.

More than 170 years ago a naval author, describing the amusements of seamen, wrote: 'Buffoonery they take singular delight in. We seldom see a ship without one or more droll fellows who, sensible of this matter, make themselves voluntary laughing-stocks to their shipmates'. Another wrote: 'The sailor loves dramatic pieces of a comic kind, with music and dancing, the whole to conclude with some song, perhaps "God Save the King", "Rule Britannia", or "The Wandering Sailor" with full chorus'.

Among favourite nautical pastimes at sea was one perhaps not quite so pleasant, concerning sport with sharks. Sir Richard Hawkins wrote of a voyage to the South Seas in 1593:

> Every day my company took more or less of them, not for what they did eat of them (for they are not held wholesome, though the Spaniards, as I have seene, doe eate them)* but to recreate themselves, and in revenge of the injuries received by them; for they live long and suffer much after they bee taken before they dye. At the tayle of one they tyed a great logge of wood; at another an empty *batizia* (small cask) well strapped; one they yoked like a hogge; from another they plucked his eyes out and so threw them into the sea. In catching two together, they bound them tayle to tayle, and so set them swimming; another with his belly slit, and his bowels hanging out, which his fellows would have every one a snatch at; with other infinite inventions to entertayne the time, and to avenge themselves, for that they deprived them of swimming, and fed on their flesh, being dead.

Another seagoing diversion, which began as a morality play in medieval times and has survived to the present day, is that of 'Crossing the Line'. It was not only on passing the Equator that such a ceremony took place, for in Dutch ships when a vessel entered the 39th parallel all those on board who had not passed before were ducked overboard from the bowsprit, unless they were prepared to redeem themselves by some kind of payment to the seamen.

> The ceremony took place in the bows of the ship, where some kind of stage had been erected, and where the principal mariners, suitably attired for the occasion, made use of a set ritual with dramatic words and action. Other writers state that the sailors were dressed as judges, and that the mummery took the character of a trial, at which the victims of the seamen's facetiousness were on evidence found guilty and sentenced to

* In later years sharks' flesh was eaten by British sailors. It formed, along with salt pork and biscuit, an ingredient for 'chowder'.

death. It was very rough humour, however, for if the sentence was not redeemed with money, wine, provisions or the like, flogging was the least of the punishments to which they became liable.*

In Spanish ships it was the custom to preface the trial of the offenders against Neptune's laws with an imitation bullfight. In Portuguese vessels the forfeits were regarded as contributions to the Church. These customs were also practised when passing the Straits of Gibraltar and the Cape of Good Hope. Parson Teonge, a seventeenth-century naval chaplain, in an account of passing through the Straits of Gibraltar in 1675, recorded that:

> Ape's Hill is a rock of great height, and extreme steep; on the top of it lives a Marabout wizard or Enchanter; and what vessel soever of the Turks goes by, gives him a gun as she goes to beg a fortunate voyage. Here everyone that hath not yet been in the Straits pays his dollar or must be ducked at the yard-arm.

But the ceremony of 'Crossing the Line', more or less in its present form, began around 1791. Guidance as to the established form of ritual to be observed in HM ships is to be found in the afore-mentioned volume *Sports and Recreation in the Royal Navy*, of which the following is a brief summary.

The ship usually stops engines at about sunset on the day before she is due to cross the Equator, and from behind a screen rigged up on the forecastle, King Neptune's messengers emerge to deliver an address of welcome to the ship 'entering Neptune's domains', at the same time summoning all novices to appear before Neptune's Court at a certain time on the following day.

On this day, King Neptune, together with Queen Amphitrite, appears, attended by the Court officials, consisting of the Clerk of the Court, the Doctor, the Barber, Neptune's police and the Bears. After a ceremonial parade round the upper deck, they take their places in the Court. The novices (officers and ratings alike) then appear, and, one at a time, take a seat where they are lathered and 'shaved' by the Barber, and given a 'pill' by the Doctor. While this is in progress, the seat is tipped up, throwing its occupant into a

---

* *The British Tar in Fact and Fiction*, Robinson.

huge canvas bath full of seawater, where he is mercilessly ducked by the Bears. The Police search out all those who try to escape the ceremony, and, at its conclusion, the Clerk of the Court issues each initiate with a certificate as proof of having become a subject of King Neptune.

Not even war conditions are allowed to interfere with custom. On 10th April 1940 Commander Robert Ryder, RN, then commanding a British 'Q-ship', hunting for U-boats and German surface raiders in the Atlantic, recorded in his private log: 'Yesterday we had our Crossing the Line ceremony, surpassing in thoroughness anything I have ever seen before!'

Crossing the Line ceremony in one of H.M. Ships. Ducking a victim.

CHAPTER XIV

Merrymaking, Measurements and Marines

Christmas Day in the Navy brings a temporary relaxation of normal work and discipline, and is an occasion for certain traditional fun and games. In the past, however, as will be seen, the seamen's festive revels were not for the squeamish.

One amusing shipboard custom which has its origins far back in history, occurs at the commencement of the captain's Christmas morning rounds. When he appears to carry out this ritual inspection, accompanied by the officers, he is met by his lower deck 'opposite number'. According to tradition this is the most junior rating in the ship, clad for the occasion in an officer's discarded uniform jacket, embellished with four chalked rings on the sleeves, an impressive looking row of imitation medals, an officer's cap boasting considerable 'scrambled egg', and, if one can be scrounged, even a sword.

Accompanying him as aide and 'chief skate' (defaulter) is the Master-at-Arms, no longer his august self, but bursting out of a bluejacket's inadequately fitting jumper and bell-bottoms, and wearing at the back of his head a disreputable sailor's cap fit only to be thrown over the side. A 'squeegee' band dressed in a variety of absurd rigs, with instruments to match, brings up the rear of the party. After gravely shaking hands to a cacophonous fanfare, the two 'captains' then proceed to inspect the gaily decorated mess decks.

This popular and traditional bit of nautical tomfoolery dates back to pagan times when it was the custom on certain festival occasions for masters to wait upon their slaves, who in turn assumed the latter's lordly role, and for various forms of junketing.

But in Britain's 'wooden wall' Navy, since there was usually little additional available in the way of seasonal fare, the men saved up their rum ration for days before Christmas in order to indulge in one glorious binge when they could temporarily forget the hardships of their daily lives. Officers usually kept well clear of the mess decks then, for the old-fashioned shipboard 'wet Christmas' was no mere children's party. In fact it was not at all unusual to find one or two corpses lying about when the decks were cleared up next day!

Samuel Leech, who served in the Navy during the Napoleonic wars, wrote disgustedly:

> At Christmastime the ship presented a scene such as I had never imagined. The men were permitted to have their 'full swing', and drunkenness ruled the ship. Nearly every man, with most of the officers, was in a state of beastly intoxication at night. Here, some were fighting but were so insensibly drunk they hardly knew whether they struck the guns or their opponents; yonder a party were singing libidinous or bacchanalian songs; while all were laughing, cursing, swearing or hallooing; confusion reigned in glorious triumph; it was the very chaos of humanity.*

On the whole, however, officers appear to have fared rather better, judging from an account of the seasonal celebrations on board HMS *Assistance* in 1675 by Parson Teonge, whom we met earlier on.

> Christmas Day wee kept thus. At four in the morning our trumpeters all doe flatt their trumpets and began at our captain's cabin, and thence to all the officers' and gentlemen's cabins, playing a levite at each cabin doore, and bidding good-morrow, wishing a merry Christmas. After they goe to their stations, viz., on the poope, and sound three levites in honour of the morning. At ten we goe to prayers and sermon. Our captain had all his officers and gentlemen to dinner with him, where wee had excellent good fayre: a ribb of beife, plumb puddings, minct pyes, etc., and plenty of good wines of severall sorts; drank healthe to the King, to our wives and friends, and ended the day with civill myrth.

More than two centuries later, Christmas Day on board HMS *Terrible* at Portsmouth in 1898, as somewhat lyrically described by her Master-at-Arms, is more typical of the way the Navy of today celebrates the season, and was certainly true in many details of the

* Quoted in *From the Lower Deck*, by Henry Baynham.

General Mess,
Royal Naval Barracks, Chatham

◼   ◼

With Best Wishes for

A Merry Christmas

◼   ◼

Christmas, 1938   New Year, 1939

General Mess menu for Christmas Day 1938, R.N. Barracks Chatham.

Breakfast

Fried Bacon, Egg and Grilled Tomatoes
Rolls and Butter
Marmalade
Tea

Dinner

Cream of Tomato Soup
Roast Turkey and Stuffing   Ham
Roast Potatoes   Brussels Sprouts
Christmas Pudding   Custard Sauce
Assorted Fruits
Nuts   Figs and Dates
Chocolates
(Beer and Mineral Waters provided from
Canteen Funds)

Tea

Rolls and Jam   Christmas Cake

Supper

Cold Roast Pork
Pickles
Hot Mince Pies
Tea or Coffee

years up to the outbreak of World War II; although since the introduction of modern victualling methods it has no longer been incumbent upon individual messes to provide their own Christmas fare. Captain's rounds, however, the waiving of normal routine, and, if in harbour, an 'open gangway' enabling men to go ashore as and when they wish, are still customary.

By Christmas Eve the spacious decks had been deftly transformed into a veritable fairyland by means of abundant supplies of evergreens, coloured lamps and flags, with which the long gangways had been decorated in lavish style, while each mess had been converted into a fairy-like alcove. Keen rivalry in mess decorations and culinary productions betwixt individual messes exists in men-of-war on this occasion.

Arboreal arches, naively adorned with amusing or significant mottoes, were erected at the entrance of each mess deck, besides several mechanically worked representations of things nautical, some of which were specially designed to ambuscade the unwary inquisitor. The interior of the ship when electrically lit up presented a transformation scene of sumptuous splendour.

On Christmas morning the tables were fairly bending with the weight of edible luxuries; the quantity provided not depending so much on the number of persons berthed in each mess, as on the length of the mess table! It is an unwritten law that every inch of space must be covered with something; the viands and fruit being neatly interspersed with photographs representing various types of feminine beauty, from the gay geisha-girl of Japan to the modest maid of Devonshire. Punctually at noon Captain Robinson, accompanied by all officers on board and several guests, and preceded by the ship's band playing 'The Roast Beef of Old England', made the customary tour round the mess decks. Stopping briefly at each mess, he exchanged the compliments of the season with the mess representative, and partook of certain delicacies from the proffered plates, which it were sacrilege to pass without due recognition of their contents. But a captain would require the digestion of an ostrich and the capacity of an elephant if he even sampled all that he feels it incumbent upon him to accept. Yet it all disappears to some mysterious place known only to a captain – and perhaps his vivacious coxswain.

The day itself stands unique from all other days of the year, for from noon routine is suspended, and a sort of topsy-turveydom exists on the Lower Deck. The petty and non-commissioned officers will suavely perform the necessary routine work; the marine drummer boy and a bluejacket boy for the nonce will supersede the sergant-major and the master-at-arms; the orders of these two embryo officials being humorously obeyed. These customs, however, and also that of carrying the principal officers round the decks after dinner, though still in vogue, are but a lingering survival of the old naval lore, which before long will collapse into obscurity. Naval Christmas Days were formerly of bacchanalian character, a form of celebration which finds but little favour with the present generation. Up till evening rounds at nine p.m., the festivities continue, when at that hour routine and discipline displace revelry and decorations.

But he was mistaken; the traditional revelry, although in considerably milder form, has not yet 'collapsed into obscurity'.

Another seasonal custom in the Navy is that of striking sixteen bells on New Year's Eve. Dating back to the introduction of bells for time-keeping on shipboard, the tradition is said to have been adopted from the Merchant Navy. Struck precisely at midnight, the first set of eight bells is for the old year, and the second for the new. And to ensure good luck for the coming twelve months, the bells must be struck by the youngest person in the ship, officer, sailor or marine.

It is rare today to hear someone called 'a son of a gun', and anyone employing this expression may be interested to learn that it is not an early Americanism, but a juicy old Royal Naval insult. The expression first came into use when women were allowed on board British warships during their brief sojourns in home ports and in ports abroad. In this respect we may again quote from the captain's orders of HRH Prince William, commanding HMS *Andromeda* in the West Indies in 1788:

Order the 8th requesting and directing the first lieutenant or commanding officer to see all strangers out of His Majesty's Ship under my command at gun-fire is by no means meant to restrain the officers and men from having either black or white women on board through the night, so long as the discipline is unhurt by the indulgence. The first lieutenant is to pay the strictest attention that, upon the likelihood of His Majesty's Ship under my command proceeding to sea, every woman is sent on shore, unless he has received instructions in that behalf from the captain.

'Scenes of profligacy and debauchery used to take place on the decks of a man-of-war. The gangways had to be kept free, and it was in the spaces between the guns that these scenes occurred.'* Hence to call a man 'a son of a gun' was equivalent to casting doubts on the legitimacy of his parentage. An old definition of a boy born as the result of a temporary mess deck liaison was that he was 'begotten in the galley and born under a gun. Every hair of his head a rope yarn, every tooth a marline spike, every finger a fish hook, and in his blood right good Stockholm tar'.

In those bad old days when little or no shore leave was given, a warship would be literally invaded by a horde of women on her arrival in harbour, when each man in the crew could choose whichever he fancied. Officers who were jealous of the reputation of their ships not infrequently refused to admit plain or ugly women, and any not suitably attired or, cosmetically, sufficiently well made up. Local boatmen often constituted themselves arbiters of judgment in this respect, rowing out only the prettiest and best dressed.

But in the seventeenth and eighteenth centuries, and even the early years of the nineteenth century, a certain number of women were legitimately – if unofficially – carried on board ship. Some captains took their wives to sea, among them one of the two brothers of Jane Austen, both of whom became admirals. One captain recommended to the Admiralty that 'a proportion of three to four women should be included to every hundred men at sea – confining this indulgence expressly to respectable married women – which could not fail to have a good effect'.

But certain senior officers objected to the practice, among them Admirals St Vincent, Nelson and Collingwood.

The wives of a few of the more trustworthy men on board

* *A Few Naval Customs, Expressions, Traditions & Superstitions*, Beckett.

Forecastle scene in an eighteenth-century British warship, showing women on board.

remained with the permission of the captain. These latter were tolerated on board partly because they were the wives of well behaved men and so themselves well behaved, and partly because they had a definite use in and after action, helping the boys to bring up powder from the magazines during battle, and nursing wounded seamen afterwards. They were not officially victualled in the ship, being expected to share their husband's allowance.*

It is from the days when women were allowed to remain on board that the term 'show a leg' is derived. Since females were exempt from turning out with the hands first thing in the morning, this call was made to check that the occupant of a hammock really was a woman entitled to enjoy the privilege of lying in for an extra half hour.

John Nicol, a press-ganged ex-merchant seaman who served in the Navy during the Revolutionary war against France, and was

* *The British Sailor*, Peter Kemp.

A rare naval General Service medal with
seven bars, awarded in 1851 to Gunner
Thomas Haines, R.N.

present in the 74-gun *Goliath* at the Battles of St Vincent and the Nile, wrote of the latter action:

> I saw little [of the battle] as my station was in the powder magazine with the Gunner. As we entered the bay we stripped to our trowsers, opened our ports, cleared, and every ship we passed gave them a broadside and three cheers. Any information we got was from the boys and women who carried the powder. The women behaved as well as the men, and got a present for their bravery ... I was much indebted to the Gunner's wife, who gave her husband and me a drink of wine every now and then which lessened our fatigue much. There were some of the women wounded and one woman belonging to Leith died of her wounds, and was buried on a small island in the bay. One woman bore a son in the heat of the action.

The names of four women actually appear in the Muster Book of the *Goliath* for this period. Widows of men killed in the action, who had helped to bandage and nurse the wounded, they were Sarah Bates, Ann Taylor, Elizabeth Moore and Mary French. Since there was then no 'Sex Discrimination Act', they were granted only two-thirds of the men's victualling allowance. In 1952 a public house in Chatham was given the name 'Trafalgar Maid' to commemorate a woman who had served in the frigate *Euryalus* at Trafalgar. For years after the action she lived in a part of the town which housed sailors and shipwrights of Nelson's day, and the story of her adventures was published in a magazine in 1837.

When in 1847 Queen Victoria ordered a medal – known as the General Service Medal – to be struck to recognise the services rendered by her fleets and armies from 1793 to 1815, one woman, Jane Townshend of HMS *Defiance*, claimed the medal and bar for Trafalgar. But although she had indeed been present at the battle, her claim was disallowed; so that, despite what legend may say on the subject, no woman actually received the medal. One recipient, however, was a man who had been born in HMS *Tremendous* only a few days before the battle of the Glorious First of June in 1794, his rating at the time being given as 'Baby'. His mother was the wife of a seaman named McKenzie, the child being appropriately christened Daniel Tremendous McKenzie.

There were also women who dressed up as men and managed to conceal their sex successfully while serving on board ship. Three such of whom records exist were Mary Ann Talbot, Anne Mills and Rebecca Johnson. As a young girl Mary Ann Talbot fell in love with an army officer, and in the name of John Taylor served overseas as his servant. After being wounded she was taken on board a French privateer. The latter was captured by a British warship, and as an 'escaped English prisoner' she served as a seaman in the Royal Navy. Since she is described as being tall and angular with long arms and 'singularly lacking in feminine grace', she presumably found it not too difficult to conceal her sex. After all, although ships' companies of those times lived pretty much cheek by jowl, there were no baths or toilets as we know them on board warships. But when she was wounded in the leg at the Glorious First of June battle, she was compelled to reveal her secret to the surgeon, and was duly discharged.

Comparatively few details are available concerning Rebecca Johnson and Anne Mills. The former is said to have actually been apprenticed to the sea at the age of thirteen by her brutal father, who had rid himself of his wife in the same way; she was believed to have been killed at the Battle of Copenhagen. The latter, who enjoyed the reputation of being 'hard-living and blood-thirsty', served under Nelson, and in hand-to-hand fighting with enemy boarders, or as a boarder herself, specialised in decapitating her opponents with one blow of her cutlass!

The sailor's day of twenty-four hours is divided into seven shifts, or periods of duty called 'watches', and the 24-hour clock has long been used at sea. In fact, it can be said that the Navy was the first to adopt this method of time-keeping in order to obviate confusion in signals. The day starts at midnight, being recorded as '0000' (the addition of the word 'hours', e.g., 0600 hours, is *not* used in the Navy as it is in the other two Services). The watches are then as follows:-

0001-0400	–	Middle
0400-0800	–	Morning
0800-1200	–	Forenoon
1200-1600	–	Afternoon

1600-1800 – First Dog
1800-2000 – Last Dog
2000-0000 – First

The reason for introducing 'Dog' watches, which are shortened to two hours each, was to provide an odd number of watches, thus giving the men different periods of duty each day. The term 'Dog' watch probably derived from 'Dodge' watch – it might even be, according to some nautical humorists, because a dog is 'curtailed'. Not inappropriately, the Middle Watch is known as the 'graveyard' watch, for then human spirits are at their lowest ebb.

The passage of time on shipboard is indicated by the striking of bells, the number struck denoting the number of half-hours which have elapsed from the beginning of the current watch. The origin of this custom is obscure, but records show that this method of denoting the time was in use as early as the thirteenth century. Since there were then no clocks in ships, the method of keeping the (approximate) time was by means of a half-hour sand glass (like an egg-timer), the bell being struck each time the glass was reversed. Columbus carried half-hour sandglasses and his log recorded a day and night as 48 *Ampolettas* or Sandglasses. Half-hour glasses were in use in the Royal Navy until late in the nineteenth century, when it was common to hear time being expressed in 'glasses', e.g., 'We should finish the job in about three glasses'. Coming on watch a few minutes before being required to take over was said to be 'flogging the glass' or 'warming the bell'.

Starting, then, at 0830 with one bell, two bells are struck at 0900, three at 0930, and so on up to eight bells at noon. The sequence is then repeated until eight bells at 1600; but only one bell is struck at 1830 because we are now in the dog watches. Two bells are struck at 1900, three at 1930, and eight once more at 2000. At sea, in the Navy at least, no more bells are struck after 2200, these being known as 'silent hours'. The practice of striking only one bell at 1830 is said to have been instituted after the naval mutiny at the Nore, because it became known that the striking of five bells in the first dog watch was to be the signal for the commencement of the mutiny on 12th May 1797. The custom has been continued ever since, and is even followed in foreign warships.

As most people know, ships progress at sea at the rate of knots;

although not, it should be emphasised, 'knots per hour'. One knot is equal to one nautical mile per hour, but this differs in length from the landsman's mile per hour. The land mile measures 1760 yards, or 5280 feet, and the nautical mile about 2000 yards, or 6080 feet, the length varying slightly with latitude. The knot became the sailor's unit of speed some four centuries ago, when Elizabethan mariners began to employ a device called the 'Common Log' to gauge the speed of their ships through the water.

This device consisted of four parts. First came the 'Log-ship', a lead-weighted wooden quadrant to act as the float. To this was secured a thin line measuring from ten to twenty fathoms in length – long enough to carry the 'log-ship' clear of the ship's wake – which was called the 'stray-line'. The logline itself was coiled on a 'log-reel', the division between this and the 'stray-line' being distinguished by a piece of coloured bunting. The logline was marked with knots at regular intervals, the distance between them bearing the same relation to a nautical mile as the number of seconds in a sand glass bears to the hour. This part of the apparatus was known as the 'log-glass', and was timed for either 14, 28 or 30 seconds.

To operate, or 'stream' the log, a sailor held up the 'log-reel', and an officer threw the 'log-ship' overboard to windward. When the bunting on the 'stray-line' reached his hand, the 'log-glass' was inverted to start the timing. The number of knots which had passed him by the time the sand ran out gave the ship's speed. Hence, despite the introduction of modern electronic devices which can show a ship's captain his vessel's speed at a glance, it is still calculated in knots and not miles per hour – even nautical ones.

The word 'log' itself derives from an even more primitive method of gauging a ship's speed: that of throwing a line-secured log of wood overboard at the bows and timing its arrival at the stern. Since the length of the ship was known, plus the time taken by the log to traverse that distance, a simple calculation gave speed through the water.

Sailors measure ropes, hawsers and depths of water in fathoms, and a fathom is six feet. Until comparatively recently the soundings marked on charts were always shown in fathoms. Some ten years ago, however, in view of the move towards adoption of the metric system in the United Kingdom, new style Admiralty charts now show depths and heights in metres. And a metre being 39.370 inches is just over half a fathom. 'The passing of the time-honoured fathom', stated the Hydrographer of the Navy in announcing the decision to make the change, 'will no doubt occasion regret in some hearts, but its replacement by the metre should present no problem to the mariner'. The regret, however, remains.

No book about naval customs and traditions would be complete without including mention of the Royal Marines – the Navy's soldiers.

First brought into existence in 1664, when King Charles II signed an Order-in-Council directing that 'Twelve hundred Land Souldjers be forthwith raysed to be in readinesse to be distributed into His Majesty's Fleets prepared for sea service', the marines have earned their proud reputation of 'the greatest Corps in the world'.

To the sailor, Marines are irreverently known as 'Bootnecks' or 'Leathernecks', the latter nickname deriving from the leathern tongue they once wore at the junction of the collar of their tunics. At that time they also wore pigtails. In the past they were also known as 'Turkeys', from the red tunics formerly worn, and 'Jollies', which was the original nickname of the Trained Bands of the City of London from which the earliest recruits were mainly drawn; and even 'Bullocks', a reference to the beefy types who largely composed the former Royal Marine Artillery.

Between 1862 and 1923 when the two arms amalgamated, the Corps comprised the Royal Marine Light Infantry, who wore a thin red distinguishing stripe down the sides of their trousers; and the Royal Marine Artillery – originally formed to take over the handling of mortars in bomb ketches – who sported a broader red stripe on their trousers. They were then known respectively – and unofficially – as 'Red' and 'Blue' Marines, from the latter having originally worn blue tunics.

The saying 'tell it to the Marines' is by no means a sneer at their alleged gullibility. It implies that if the Marines, who have served their country in every part of the world, will believe a story, then it must be true. Also any reference to 'Horse Marines' should not be taken to be derisory. In 1861 the Royal Marines did indeed provide a mounted detachment to help in quelling troubles in Mexico. During the campaigns in Egypt and the Sudan in 1882 and 1884, Marines not only served in ships and river gunboats, but, suitably mounted on 'ships of the desert', one company formed part of a special Guards Camel Regiment. Wrote Sergeant Eagle of this experience:

> *I've rode in a ship, I've rode in a boat,*
> *I've rode on a railway train.*
> *I've rode in a coach, I've rode a moke,*
> *And I hope to ride one again.*
> *But I'm riding now an animal*
> *A Marine never rode before,*
> *Rigged up in spurs and pantaloons,*
> *As one of the Camel Corps.*

And horse riding is included in the new entry training of Marine officers today.

One of the old customs concerning Marines on board ship is that normally they are messed between the ship's company and the officers. This practice dates back to the naval mutinies of 1797 when Admiral the Earl of St Vincent, who held the rank of General in the Corps, ordered that the sea soldiers, for whom he always had the highest regard, should mess between the officers and the sailors. Only thus could he ensure that quarterdeck authority would be upheld.

Royal Marines come under the Army when ashore and the Ministry of Defence (Navy) as soon as they board a warship. But even in ships their living quarters are not referred to as messes – they are always the 'barracks'. In addition to the maintenance of their own part of the ship, manning boats, and performing many of the normal tasks of the sailors, Marines carry out sentry duties, take charge of the ship's keys and small arms, act as officers' servants and admirals' orderlies; they form guards and landing parties, and man a proportion of the ship's armament. Whenever the Royal Navy is on parade, the Royal Marines form part of the naval contingent.

On board ships carrying a Royal Marine detachment, the sergeant-major still performs his old-time duty of reminding the navigating officer to wind the chronometers, reporting to the captain each morning at sea: 'Chronometers wound, sir'. This custom is a hangover from the early days of these nautical timekeepers, whose makers specified that they should be wound at stated times only. Since the sergeant-major had little to do with the ship's routine, he was considered to be the most reliable man to remember this important duty.

One of the most impressive and popular 'turns' given for the benefit of the public by Royal Marine bands is Beating Retreat, which has drawn enthusiastic crowds all over the world. Beating Retreat is the survival of a custom which dates back at least to the year 1690, and has been defined as 'A beat of the Drum at the firing of the evening gun; at which the drum major with all the drums of the battalion except such as are upon duty beats from the camp colours on the right to those on the left on the parade of encampment; the drums of all the guards beat also; the trumpets at the same time sounding at the head of their respective troops. This is to warn the soldiers to forbear firing and the sentinels to challenge till the break of day, that the reveille is beat. The retreat is likewise called "setting the watch".' In fortified places it was also the signal for the inhabitants to come in before the gates were shut.

Finally, the Royal Marines enjoy one special privilege not conferred upon the Royal Navy. They may march through the City of London with bayonets fixed, colours flying and band playing at any time they please. This ancient privilege, shared with certain Army regiments, originated in the days of Charles II. After his restoration in 1660 he disbanded nearly the whole of the Army, with the exception of the King's Regiment of Foot Guards (now the Grenadier Guards), the Holland Regiment (The Buffs), and the Duke of York's Regiment (the Royal Marines). By the issue of Warrants he authorised the officers of these regiments to raise recruits 'by beat of drum' within the City, and the Lord Mayor's permission was given. Recruiting was done by marching through the City streets with colours flying, drums beating and bayonets fixed to attract attention.

That the civic authorities have long acknowledged the right of Her Majesty's 'Jollies' to exercise the privilege is illustrated by an incident which took place in 1746. A detachment of Royal Marines were drumming their way along Cheapside on a recruiting drive when a City magistrate hurried up and ordered them to 'cease interrupting the civil repose'.

'Sir,' cried the officer in charge of the detachment indignantly, 'we are Marines!'

'Oh, sir', came the apologetic response, 'I beg pardon. I did not know it. Pray continue your route as you please'.

But the civic fathers of our capital city would not dream of banning their streets to the men of the Royal Navy. If the Senior Service wishes to be accorded the privilege at any time, it has only to ask.

CHAPTER XV

Unwillingly to the Breaker's

Even in this modern sophisticated age there are sailors who believe that ships are sentient, living creations, possessing souls of their own from the time they slide down the ways. They are also firmly convinced that when a ship is condemned to the breaker's yard, the beating heart of her engines stilled for ever, cabins stripped and bare, mess decks silent and empty yet peopled with ghosts, her spirit comes to life and actively rebels against such a fate.

The more prosaic-minded may ridicule the notion, yet it is a curious fact that many warships on their way to an ignominious end in the scrapyard have broken free of their towing craft in bad spells of weather which have suddenly and unaccountably sprung up, and either foundered or stranded themselves beyond possibility of subsequent salvage.

The grounding in Portsmouth harbour of the battleship *Vanguard* on her way to the breaker's in 1960 has already been mentioned. In April 1947 the 31,000-ton battleship *Warspite*, 'grand old lady' of the Mediterranean Fleet for most of World War II, and a veteran of Jutland, left Portsmouth to be broken up on the Clyde. She had been bought by a firm of shipbreakers, and was in tow of two of their most powerful tugs, with eight of their men on board the empty battleship to tend the towlines. On the way down Channel a fierce gale suddenly sprang up, and presently the towline between one of the tugs and their reluctant charge parted. After a long and tiring struggle, the tug crew managed to get another line on board, and it was decided to anchor in Mount's Bay in Cornwall until the weather moderated.

But the spirit of the *Warspite* seemed determined that she should never reach the Clyde. In foaming seas, the old battleship persistently dragged her anchor, inching closer and closer to the shore. Bumping heavily over a rock, she continued to drag herself towards Prussia Cove. For three days and three nights the tug crews fought to haul the recalcitrant vessel back into deep water. But she would have none of it. At last the exhausted men were compelled to give up, and with considerable difficulty the Mousehole lifeboat took off the towing crew. The *Warspite* finally had to be abandoned as a total wreck.

In the previous year no fewer than six warships on their way to the scrapyards had revolted against this form of death sentence. Four of them were submarines with distinguished war records. In January the *Safari*, which had performed brilliant work in the Mediterranean, decided that a future as razor blades was not for her. She broke away from her tug near Portland and sank.

In the following month the *United*, on her way to the breaker's with a naval steaming crew from Lissahally, in Northern Ireland, sprang a leak after eight hours at sea. While being battered by heavy weather off the Outer Hebrides, both engines failed and her wireless broke down. The destroyer *Fame* was sent to her aid and managed to get a towline to her, but during the next twelve hours this continually snapped. The frigate *Loch Fada* then arrived and also tried towing. But the *United* seemed bent on her own destruction. There were, however, naval men on board, and eventually they got one engine going again. Escorted by destroyer and frigate, the submarine finally regained the shelter of Lissahally, thus postponing, for a time at least, her scheduled end.

In December the submarine *Truant* made a bid to escape the breaker's yard. In a Channel gale and heavy seas, she broke away from her tug, and without a man on board, proudly rode out the gale. But in calmer weather she was recovered, to end her days in a scrapyard. Earlier, in May, the 4850-ton cruiser *Diomede*, on her way to be broken up in the Clyde, was taken by her tug for temporary shelter in Mount's Bay. Heavy seas and a strong wind combined to aid the cruiser to break away from her captor, and she impaled herself on rocks not far from the future graveyard of the *Warspite*. But she was successfully towed clear, patched up, and dragged off to become an anonymous pile of scrap steel. The fleet minesweeper *Saltburn* was another post-war candidate for the shipbreaker that refused to accept her fate. Off the north Devon coast she broke loose from her tug and piled herself up on the rocks at Hartland Point.

In 1949 HMS *Ajax*, one of the victors of the River Plate battle, whose name was adopted for a new town in Ontario, Canada, its streets named after certain officers and men who had served in the ship during the action, tried to rebel against the end decreed for her by the Admiralty. En route to the breaker's, she ran aground on mudbanks at the mouth of the River Usk, and for more than a week defied all the efforts of a veritable fleet of tugs to shift her.

Three years later the 19,200-ton former Brazilian battleship *Sao Paulo* made world headline news when she mysteriously disappeared in mid-Atlantic while being towed from Rio de Janeiro to be ·broken up at Greenock. In charge of two powerful ocean-going tugs, she had reached the vicinity of the Azores when a gale blew up. While the little flotilla was struggling against mountainous seas, the old battleship broke adrift and vanished. For days a widespread sea and air search was carried on, but no trace was found of the ship or the 8-man towing crew she carried, and the search had finally to be abandoned. A subsequent official enquiry produced no real solution to the mystery.

More recently, the 50,000-ton aircraft carrier *Eagle* en route to a breaker's yard at Loch Ryan, near Stranraer, ran aground on a sandbank three hundred yards from her final destination. She had made the journey from Devonport docilely enough in tow of three Ministry of Defence tugs. But as soon as they handed over the tow to civilian tugs, the doomed carrier showed her defiance.

These are just some of the many instances of warships destined for scrapping coming to grief on their last voyages, and for each it is possible to find a reasonable theory to account for the occurrence. But to the true, dyed-in-the-wool mariner there can be only one explanation.

The following two Prayers and Psalm are included as a tailpiece because they have become part of centuries-old naval tradition.

Sir Francis Drake's prayer on the day he entered Cadiz in 1587 to 'singe the King of Spain's beard', and thereby compelled the postponement for twelve months of the sailing of the Spanish Armada against England:

> O Lord God when thou givest to thy servants to endeavour any great matter, grant us also to know that it is not the beginning, but the continuing of the same, until it be thoroughly finished, which yieldeth the true glory; through Him that for the finishing

of thy work laid down his life, our Redeemer, Jesus Christ.
Amen.

Lord Nelson's prayer on the eve of Trafalgar, 1805:

May the great God, whom I worship, grant to my Country, and
for the benefit of Europe in general, a great and glorious victory,
and may no misconduct in anyone tarnish it, and may humanity
after victory be the predominant feature in the British Fleet.
For myself individually I commit my life to Him that made me,
and may His Blessing alight on my endeavours for serving my
Country faithfully. To Him I resign myself – and the just cause
which is entrusted to me to defend. Amen. Amen. Amen.

The sailor's psalm:

They that go down to the sea in ships, and occupy their business
in great waters. These men see the works of the Lord; and his
wonders in the deep. For at his word the stormy wind ariseth:
which lifteth up the waves thereof. They are carried up to the
heavens, and down again to the deep: their soul melteth away
because of the trouble. They reel to and fro and stagger like a
drunken man: and are at their wits' end. So when they cry unto
the Lord in their trouble: he delivereth them out of their distress.
For he maketh the storm to cease: so that the waves thereof are
still. Then they are glad, because they are at rest: and so he
bringeth them unto the haven where they would be.

Appendix I

A selected glossary of terms and expressions in common use in the Royal Navy, some of which have also become part of everyday speech on shore.

Avast: Stop; hold fast.

Adrift: Broken away from moorings; missing; absent over leave or from place of duty.

Belay: Make fast or secure, rope; (colloquially) countermand an order.

Blue Peter: A blue flag with a white square in the centre. Originally a signal for the general recall of officers and men to their ships. Used today to signify the imminent departure of a merchant ship from port.

'Brocky': Spotty-faced.

Brow: The gangway between ship and shore when a vessel is lying alongside, *not* 'gangplank', which is the means of passage between individual ships when they are alongside each other.

Bulkhead: Partitions by means of which internal compartments are formed; the transverse watertight divisions in the interior of a ship.

'Between the Devil and the Deep Sea': In wooden ships the 'devil' was a large deck seam near the gunwale. To be working between this and the waterline was to be in a precarious position.

'Bitter End': In a sailing warship (and merchantman) the 'bitts' were wooden centre-line bollards to which the anchor cable and certain ropes were belayed. When they were run out almost to the limit, they were said to be nearing the 'bitter end'.

'By and Large': Sailing terms. 'By' meant close-hauled; 'Large' running free. Sailing under any condition of wind.

Complement: The entire company of a warship, officers and men.

'Clew up': To bring to an end. Originally to draw up the lower ends of the sails to the yards by their clews.

'Chock-a-block': Originally 'block and block'. The state of a tackle when its standing and moving blocks are hauled close together. (Colloquially) bored, or fed up; 'Chocker'. (See also 'Two blocks'.)

'Chuck-up': Any form of nautical encouragement, or applause.

Displacement: The actual weight of a vessel represented by the number of tons' weight of water she displaces when loaded with fuel, water, stores, ammunition, and crew on board.

'Dead Marine': Empty bottle. Said of the latter that, like a Marine, it has done its duty and is ready to do it again.

'Dummy Run': An exercise or rehearsal.

'Dished up': Disrated; punished.

Davy Jones: Strictly 'Duffy' Jones, or ghost of Jonah. 'Duffy' is an old English word for ghost.

'Doggo': Plain-featured; ugly.

'Drink': A reprimand, or 'bottle'. (See 'a dose from the foretopman's bottle'); also the sea.

'Drip': To grumble or complain.

'Flag Jack': The Flag Lieutenant; also 'Flags'.

'Flannel': An ingratiating manner; bluff; an insincere speech or 'pep' talk; equivalent of 'soft soap'.

'Flap': Unnecessary haste; confusion; 'panic stations'.

'Flog the Cat': To complain.

Flotsam: Goods or material found floating in the sea, as opposed to *Jetsam*, which has been thrown overboard, or jettisoned.

Fo'c'sle: Foreshortening of forecastle. In olden times ships had fighting platforms, or 'castles', at bow and stern; the latter being known as the 'after-castle'.

'Friday While': Long weekend leave from Friday to Monday.

'Gannet': Any individual with an insatiable appetite for food.

'Gash': Spare; superfluous; said of leftovers of food.

'Green Rub': An undeserved rebuke.

'Guff': Nonsense.

'Head down, to get one's: To sleep; to have a 'caulk'. Dates from the Grand Fleet days of World War I.

'Heads': The lavatories in a ship. Originally platforms on either side of the stem, or 'beakhead', were used as latrines.

'Jack Strop': A truculent, trouble-making individual.

'Jankers': Punishment; extra work; stoppage of leave.

'Lash Up': To stand treat.

'Lined Up': Paraded as a defaulter.

'Make One's Number': Report for duty, or introduce oneself in a new mess.

'Maltese Lace': The frayed edges of clothing.

'Muckstick': Rifle; inverted form of 'musket'.

'Mudhook': The anchor.

'Oggin': The sea; perversion of 'hogwash'; also the 'pond', 'drink', 'ditch'.

'Oppo': Opposite number; friend; pal.

'One Long Coal Ship': An expression meaning any dreary and arduous occupation. Dates back to the days of coal-fired warships in the Navy, when something like a thousand tons of coal at a time had to be

embarked from a collier by the men themselves. This involved sacking the coal, hoisting it inboard, weighing it, and stowing it in the bunkers. All hands, including officers, had to take part in the evolution of 'Coal ship'.

'Pea Doo Medal': The Long Service & Good Conduct Medal. 'Pea doo' is naval slang for pea soup, and thus associated with the award of certain decorations which are said to 'come up with the rations'. The Long Service & Good Conduct Medal is sardonically alleged by the cynical to be awarded for 'fifteen years of undiscovered crime!'

'Pier Head Jump': A sudden draft to a seagoing ship; a last minute move.

'Poodle-Faker': A wardroom socialite.

Porthole: Circular aperture in a ship's side; properly a 'scuttle'.

'Push The Boat Out': Stand a round of drinks.

Port: The left-hand side of a ship looking forward. Formerly 'larboard' from the Italian *laborda*. The change was made in the British Navy by Admiralty order of 22nd November 1844.

'Q.D.': The quarterdeck.

'Queen Bee': The senior WRNS officer.

'Rattle, in the': Placed in the report for a misdemeanour; 'scoring a rattle'. Possibly from 'to rail at in a noisy manner'; to be shaken like a pea in a rattle.

'Royal': Vocative for a Royal Marine.

'Rub': A loan.

'Rub Up': A refresher course.

Starboard: The right-hand side of a ship looking forward.

Sick Bay: Originated early in the nineteenth century as the 'Sick Berth'. In 1798 Admiral the Earl of St Vincent, when Commander-in-Chief in the Mediterranean, directed a 'sick berth' to be prepared in each ship of the line, to be situated under the forecastle 'with a roundhouse enclosed for the use of the sick'. The rounded shape of the bow resembled the bay window in a room. In 1884 a Sick Berth branch was formed to serve in shore hospitals, trained in the care of the 'Sick and Hurt of her Majesty's Navy'.

'Squeegee Band': Composed of instruments not usually found in a band, e.g. Jew's harp; mouth-organ; comb and paper, etc.

'Scran': Food.

'Scribe', or *'Scratch':* Any Writer rating.

'Scull': To wander about aimlessly.

'Smack It About': Exhortation to get a move on.

'Smigget': Good-looking.

'Square' or 'Soft Number': An easy job or appointment.

'Sprog': New entry.

'Steaming Covers': 'Long johns' or long underwear. Originated in the early days of steam in the British Navy, when 'spit and polish' captains protected the painted lower masts of their ships with canvas covers against blackening by smuts from the funnel.

'Tally': Name.

'Taut Hand': A good, all-round sailor whom everyone respects.

'Topsides': On deck; aloft.

'Trick': A spell on watch, e.g., the helmsman 'takes a trick' at the wheel.

'Two Blocks': When the two blocks of a tackle are hauled close together so that no further movement is possible; (colloquially) to reach the limit of one's patience and endurance.

'Urk', 'Fowl', 'Skate': A general 'bad hat'; a rating always in trouble.

'Weed on, to have a': To air a grievance.

'Wren-o': A Wren Officer; female 'N.O'.

'Wrennery': WRNS Quarters.

'Zizz': Sleep; formerly 'caulk' from lying on the caulked deck planking.

Appendix II

The following lines, entitled 'The Laws of the Navy', first appeared in the *Army & Navy Gazette* for 23rd July 1898, the author apparently preferring to remain anonymous under the initial 'J'. Although out of date on certain points of technical detail, e.g., 'Harveyised belt' (an armoured belt for warships made of face-hardened steel, a process invented by H.A. Harvey), the principles enunciated in these lines probably still hold good. They are therefore reproduced as a matter of interest.

THE LAWS OF THE NAVY

Now these are the laws of the Navy, unwritten and varied they be,
And he that is wise will observe them, going down in his ship to the sea;
As naught may outrun the destroyer, even so with the law and its grip;
For the strength of a ship is the Service, and the strength of the Service
    the ship.

Take heed what ye say of your rulers, be your words spoken softly or
    plain,
Lest a bird of the air tell the matter, and so ye shall hear it again.
If ye labour from morn until even and meet with reproof for your toil,
It is well; that the gun may be humbled, the compressor must check the
    recoil.
On the strength of one link in the cable dependeth the might of the chain,
Who knows when *thou* may'st be tested? So live that thou bearest the
    strain.

When the ship that is tired returneth, with the signs of the sea showing
    plain,
Men place her in dock for a season, and her speed she reneweth again;
So shalt thou lest perchance thou grow weary in the uttermost parts of
    the sea,
Pray for leave for the good of the Service, as much and as oft as may be.

Count not upon certain promotion, but rather to gain it aspire,
Though the sightline shall end on the target, there cometh perchance a
  misfire.:

Canst follow the track of the dolphin, or tell where the sea swallows
  roam?
Where leviathan taketh his pastime, what ocean he calleth his home?
Even so with the words of thy rulers, and the orders those words shall
  convey;
Every law is naught beside this one: 'Thou shall not criticise but obey'.
Saith the wise: 'Now may I know their purpose', then act without
  wherefore and why;
Stays the fool but one moment to question, and the chance of his life
  passeth by.
If ye win through an African jungle unmentioned at home in the press,
Heed it not; no man seeth the piston, but it driveth the ship none the
  less.

Do they growl? It is well, be thou silent, so that the work goeth forward
  amain;
Lo! the gun throws her shot to a hairsbreadth and shouteth, yet none
  shall complain.
Do they growl and the work be retarded? It is ill, speak whatever their
  rank;
The half loaded gun also shouteth, but can she pierce armour with
  blank?

Doth the paintwork make war with the funnels? Do the decks to the
  cannon complain?
Nay, they know that some soap and a scraper unites them as brothers
  again.
So ye, being Heads of Departments, do your growl with a smile on your
  lip,
Lest ye strive and in anger be parted, and lessen the might of your ship.

Dost deem that thy vessel needs gilding, and the dockyard forbear to
  supply,
Place thy hand in thy pocket and gild her; there be those who have risen
  thereby.
Dost think in a moment of anger, 'tis well with thy seniors to fight?
They prosper who burn in the morning the letters they wrote overnight;
For some there be shelved and forgotten, with nothing to thank for their
  fate,

But that on a mere half sheet of foolscap, a fool 'had the honour to
state' ...

If the fairway be crowded with shipping, beating homeward the
harbour to win,
It is meet lest any should suffer, the steamers pass cautiously in;
So thou, when thou nearest promotion, and the peak that is gilded is
nigh,
Give heed to thy words and thine actions lest others be wearied thereby.
It is ill for the winners to worry, take thy fate as it comes with a smile,
And when thou art safe in the harbour, they will envy but may not
revile.

Uncharted the rocks that surround thee, take heed that the channels
thou learn,
Lest thy name serve to buoy for another that shoal the Courts-Martial
return.
Tho' a Harveyised belt may protect her, the ship bears the scar on her
side;
It is well if the Court shall acquit' thee, t'were best had'st thou never
been tried.
As the wave rises clear to the hawse-pipe, washes aft and is lost in the
wake,
So shall ye drop astern, all unheeded, such time as the law ye forsake.

J.

Bibliography

Beckett, Commander W.N.T., MVO, DSC, RN; *A Few Naval Customs, Expressions, Traditions, and Superstitions*, Gieves, 1931.

Boteler, Captain Nathaniel: *Boteler's Dialogues*, Navy Records Socy. 1929.

Bullocke, J.G.: *Sailors' Rebellion*, Eyre & Spottiswood, 1938.

Falconer, *Marine Dictionary*, 1789.

Field, C.: *Britain's Sea Soldiers* (2 vols) Lyceum Press, Liverpool, 1924.

Gilby, Thomas: *Britain At Arms*, Eyre & Spottiswood, 1953.

Grover, Col. G.W.M., RM: *A Short History of the Royal Marines*, Gale & Polden, 1944.

Hampshire, A. Cecil: *The Royal Navy Since 1945*, Wm. Kimber, 1975.

Hampshire, A. Cecil: *Tercentenary of the Royal Marines*, 1964.

Kemp, Commander, P.K. RN: *The British Sailor – A Social History*, Dent, 1970.

Lewis, Michael: *The Navy of Britain*, Allen & Unwin, 1948.

Masefield, John: *Sea Life in Nelson's Time*, Methuen, 1937.

Moore, Dr J.J.: *The British Mariner's Vocabulary*, 1801.

Moulton, Major-Gen. J.L., RM: *The Royal Marines*, Leo Cooper, 1972.

Oman, Prof. Charles: *History of England*, Edward Arnold, 1895.

Parkinson, Prof. C. Northcote: *Portsmouth Point*, Liverpool University Press, 1948.

Protheroe, Ernest: *The British Navy*, Geo. Routledge & Sons, 1915.

Robinson, Commander C.N., RN: *The British Tar in Fact & Fiction*, Harper & Bros. 1909.

Robinson, Commander C.N., RN: *The British Fleet*

Smyth, Admiral W.H.: *The Sailors' Word Book*, 1867.

Trevelyan, Prof. G.M.: *English Social History*, Longmans 1942.

Index